THE TENURE OF PAROCHIAL PROPERTY *in* THE UNITED STATES OF AMERICA

A DISSERTATION

Submitted to the Faculty of Canon Law, Catholic University of America, in partial fulfilment of its requirements for the Degree of Doctor of Canon Law.

BY

CHESTER JOSEPH BARTLETT, A.M., LL.B., J.C.L.
Priest of the Diocese of Cleveland.

Washington, D. C.
1926

Nihil Obstat:

✠ THOMAS JOSEPH SHAHAN, S.T.D., Censor Deputatus.

Imprimatur:

✠ MICHAEL J. CURLEY, D. D., Archiepiscopus Baltimorensis.

Washington, D. C., May 18, 1926.

FOREWORD

"Almost all, if not all, the questions mooted in the civil courts of this country (the United States) relating to church polity, discipline, officers or members, have arisen incidentally in controversies respecting church property."[1]

The present thesis, in an attempt to lay bare the raison d'être of this curious fact, discusses the canonical and civil subjects of ownership in parish property. Dealing, of necessity, with numerous principles of ecclesiastical, civil and municipal law, both public and private, it makes no pretense to an exhaustive treatment of any particular point. Correct orientation rather than breadth of scope is its objective. A common fault of some of the most scholarly works on Canon Law, as on Justice and Rights, is, that they confine their discussion of the civil law to the codified systems of Continental Europe, and neglect the peculiar genius of the common law of English speaking countries. It is hoped that the present effort, meagre as it is, may demonstrate the value of comparative studies in American and Canon Law.

As the thesis is intended primarily for students of canon law, commentaries on municipal law, and private collections of cases have been quoted in preference to statute books and state reports which are not accessible to the average reader.

The writer desires, on this occasion to express his gratitude to the Right Reverend Joseph Schrembs, D.D., Bishop of Cleveland, through whose kindness he was directed to the Catholic University of America. He also gratefully acknowledges the value assistance given him, by his illustrious professors, and by the learned members of the legal profession, whose opinions he has incorporated into this monograph.

[1] Chief Justice Strong, *Relations of Civil Law to Church Polity*, 40.

CONTENTS

CHAPTER I.

General View of the Question.

THE most important canons governing the tenure of ecclesiastical property may be summed up in a few words. The Catholic Church, and the Apostolic See are moral persons by divine law, and have an innate right, independent of any civil power, to acquire, to hold, and to administer temporal goods.[1] Single churches, and any other moral persons possessing juridical personality by ecclesiastical authority have a similar right, governed by the regulations of the sacred canons.[2] Dominion over temporal goods under the supreme authority of the Holy See, resides in the moral person that legitimately acquired them.[3]

If these canons were recognized by the laws of the United States, it would be comparatively easy to apply them; but the matter is complicated by an apparent conflict of laws on two important points:

(1) The very notion of tenure excludes ownership that is independent of civil authority.

(2) The Church is not recognized, under the laws of the United States, as a corporation having civil rights.

"An in English-speaking countries," says Taunton,[4] "the state claims supreme dominion over all property, it is necessary to modify in practice, the active assertion of the inherent rights of the Church over ecclesiastical property; and for material safety, to observe the civil laws. The State refuses to recognize the Church as an actual corporation with the power of holding property in her own name; hence, the civil power deals only with specific individuals. . . . The Church has no desire to provoke a conflict with the civil power about ecclesiastical property."

While it is true that Taunton is dealing ex professo

[1] Canon 100, Canon 1495, § 1.

[2] Ibid.

[3] Canon 1499, § 2.

[4] *The Law of the Church*, 310.

with the law of England, it is equally true that English law is historically the basis of our own.[5] It is not surprising, therefore, to find that the law of property in the United States is influenced to some extent by the property law of England. The doctrine of tenure in England is a vestige of Feudalism, under which all the land of England was "holden, mediately, or immediately of the king who is styled the lord paramount, or above all,"[6] and although the title to land in the United States is considered allodial, and the tenure free and common socage, the law of real property in this country is still encrusted with certain feudal notions.[7] This is particularly noticeable in the doctrine of escheat, and in the right of eminent domain.[8]

The refusal of the United States to recognize the corporate existence of the Church is a technical question which will require special treatment,[9] but it may be traced to the fact that under the common law of England the so-called Concession Theory of corporations is followed. "The corporation is, and must be the creature of the State. Into its nostrils the State must breathe the breath of a fictitious life, for otherwise it would be no animated body, but individualistic dust."[10]

While the Church is not directly recognized under the laws of the United States, she still possesses a large measure of freedom. This freedom comes to her indirectly. From the standpoint of municipal law, it is the freedom, not of the Church, but of the people of the United States, possessing, under the federal and state constitutions the right to practice their religion without interference,[11] and to bind, or be bound, through contractual obligations, in a natural, or corporate capacity.[12] Catholics may therefore hold prop-

---

[5] Kent, *Commentaries,* I, 473.

[6] Blackstone, *Commentaries,* II, 59.

[7] Kent, *Commentaries,* III, 488, 489.

[8] Ibid. II, 388, 389, 423, 424.

[9] "Such recognition is given to the Church in our Island possessions by virtue of a treaty with Spain." . . . Zollmann, *American Civil Church Law,* 47.

[10] Gierke-Maitland: *Political Theories of the Middle Ages,* Translator's Introduction, p. xxx; Blackstone, *Commentaries,* I, 472.

[11] Kent, *Commentaries,* II, 35.

[12] Ibid, I, 413–423.

erty in any capacity recognized by law; but the law will, as a rule, look only to the rights of those persons in whose name the property is held. Hence, the problem in this thesis is one of personality. In what legal person, natural or artificial, is it advisable for Catholics to vest the property rights of their Church in various parts of the United States?

At first blush the answer to this question would seem to be quite simple. Since under the laws of the Church all property is supposed to be holden through a *persona moralis,* it would seem advisable for each individual church to incorporate, under the laws of its respective state. There would then exist a number of corporations, subject, in every way, to the laws of the Church, and recognized by the laws of each individual state. But, in point of fact, this condition is not always possible. Corporations in the United States are permitted only for certain definite purposes. Not every state permits ecclesiastical corporations, and those which do permit them will sometimes restrict their activities in such a way as to render incorporation undesirable from the viewpoint of canon law.

On this account, Catholics in the United States have at various times and in various places been forced to hold Church property in other than corporate capacity, and the Third Plenary Council of Baltimore, as will be seen later, outlined a number of systems of tenure that would be considered satisfactory in places where the corporate system is either impossible or undesirable.

To inquire into the nature of these various systems, and to discuss in a general, way how the Church, in conformity with her own private law, is able to function under the private law of the United States, is the object of this thesis. But since this thesis properly falls within the scope of public ecclesiastical law, some of the more important principles of public ecclesiastical law will first be discussed, primary consideration being given to the property rights of the Church, and to the personality in which these rights reside.

CHAPTER II.

Property Rights of the Church.

The Codex Iuris Canonici sets down the principle that the Catholic Church and the Apostolic See have an innate right, independent of any civil power, to acquire, to possess, and to administer temporal goods for the attainment of their respective ends.

Canon 1495.

§ 1. Ecclesia Catholica et Apostolica Sedes nativum ius habent libere et independenter a civili potestate acquirendi, retinendi et administrandi bona temporalia ad fines sibi proprios prosequendos.

This right, as Moulart[1] points out, is grounded on the natural law, on the positive law of God and on the practice of Christians through the ages.

1. Natural Law.—Abstracting from the fact of revelation, it is a duty incumbent on civil society to foster the external and public worship of God.[2] This follows from the fact that God, who is the author of individual men, is also the author of civil society; for, in making man, He made him a social being and thus virtually created society.[3] "Homines enim communi societate coniuncti nihilo sunt minus in Dei potestate, quam singuli: neque minorem, quam singuli, gratiam Deo societas debet, quo auctore coaluit, cuius nutu conservatur, cuius beneficio innumerabilem bonorum quibus affluit, copiam accepit."[4] Even if God had not established a definite form of worship, each individual would still be obliged to worship Him in whatever manner the individual conscience should dictate.[5]

---

[1] *L'Eglise et L'Etat,* 555.

[2] Tanquerey, *Synopsis Theologiae Dogmaticae,* I, 102.

[3] Catherin, *Philosophia Moralis,* 337, . . .

[4] Leo XIII, ep. encycl., *"Immortale Dei,"* Nov. 1, 1885, § 3 . . . *Fontes,* n. 592.

[5] Tanquerey, *Synopsis Theologiae Dogmaticae,* I, 95 . . .

This obligation would imply a corresponding right—a God-given right which society would be bound to respect. Therefore, if a certain group of individuals were led by conscience to form a religious association, they would be exercising a natural right; and if temporal goods were necessary for the maintenance of their association, they would have a natural right to possess and use these goods, a right which civil society would, in justice, have to acknowledge. Moreover, if they placed one individual at the head of their association, and vested this individual with certain property rights, these rights would, per se, be independent of civil authority.

The application of this argument is manifest. Even if the Catholic Church were not divinely established, both she and the Pope would, in the absence of any other divinely established religion, have the right mentioned in Canon 1495.

II. Divine Positive Law.—The Catholic Church, however, is not an association existing merely in virtue of the natural law. She is a perfect society established by Jesus Christ for the salvation of men, and the only society through which Almighty God teaches unadulterated truth, and conveys the fruits of Christ's redemption, through outward signs, to a sadly indigent world. She has a constitution given to her by her Divine Founder establishing a form of government that is at the same time monarchical and hierarchical, and essentially visible. She has a sacramental and sacrificial system requiring ministers, and places of worship, and a mission of charity which cannot be fulfilled without substantial means and unhampered freedom.

One cannot assert that the State has a right to prevent the Church from acquiring, holding, and using temporal goods, without implying that God has contradicted Himself. Since God gave the Church a definite mission, He must have given her the right to whatever means are necessary for the fulfilment of this mission. But it is evident that the acquisition, the use, and the free disposition of temporal goods are necessary if the Church is to fulfill her mission. Therefore, God gave the Church the right to temporal possessions. Now, whatever rights civil society possesses, she gets from God, since civil society is a natural society. But if God were to give the Church the right to temporal goods, and give the State the right to interfere with the possession and use of these goods, He would plainly be contradicting Himself.

Nor can it be said that the claim of the Church curtails the temporal power. There need be no conflict of rights, if each society keeps within its proper sphere of activity, and, where one society deems it desirable that the other make certain concessions, a concordat is always possible.

III. Practice of Christians Through the Ages.—It was customary among the nations of antiquity to recognize the dominion of God over the things of the earth and to set aside sacred property as the patrimony of religion.[6] In ancient Rome, for example, res sacrae, or things dedicated to the gods, were outside the scope of private ownership.[7]

It is therefore not surprising to find that the Christians followed this practice. In the time of Christ, Judas carried the common purse,[8] and later on the Apostles had a common fund formed by the free-will offerings of the faithful, and used for the support of the Church and for other charitable purposes.[9]

Even during the days of persecution the Christians continued this practice. Eusebius is authority for the fact that in the time of Pope Cornelius (251–253) the Christians in Rome alone supported one hundred and fifteen clerics and fifteen hundred indigent, besides sending assistance to the needy in other places.[10] It is also certain that the early Christians possessed real property, though there is a controversy as to the exact capacity in which they held it.[11] The more probable opinion seems to be that the Christians took advantage of the privileges which the Romans extended to Burial Societies, and vested the title

---

[6] Moulart, *L'Eglise et L'Etat,* 559.

[7] Sohm-Ledlie, *The Institutes of Roman Law,* 102, 103.

[8] John, 12, 6.

[9] Acts, 4, 32–34.

[10] *Hist. Eccl.* vi, 43—MPG, xx, 622.

[11] Marucchi: *Elements d'Archeologie Chretienne*, 117, . . . Ferrini, C., *Pandette,* n. 74.

to their various holdings in societies of this kind which they formed among themselves.[12]

From the time of the Edict of Milan (313), not only the fact of possession, but the recognition of the right to possess is beyond dispute. In addition to restoring Church property that had been confiscated under earlier emperors, Constantine actually legislated in favor of the Church, approving her right to acquire property, and rendering its acquisition easier.[13] Other emperors, particularly Theodosius and Justinian, followed his example, and in the Corpus Iuris Civilis there are numerous passages attesting the fact that the property rights of the Church were not only recognized, but, in some instances, exceptionally favored.[14]

In the various states that were carved out of the ancient territory of the Romans the same was the case. The Church not only held property, but in many instances enjoyed special favors, such as the right to take by will, immunity from taxation, restitutio in integrum, etc.[15]

That the nations took it for granted that the Church held property in her own right, and not by mere sufferance of the State, would seem to follow from the fact that the Church, on the one hand, never asked the State to confer such a right, and that the State, on the other hand, never even dreamed of the necessity of conferring it.[16]

This conclusion is supported by various legislative enactments. As early as the Sixth Century, in the contest between Pope Symmachus and Theodoric, the right to interfere in the administration of Church property was denied the laity,[17] and priests and deacons subscribing to such interference were anathematized.[18] In the Ninth Century Church property was considered by the Emperors as the patrimony of the poor, and they denied to themselves and their successors the right to alienate it.[19] Excommunications were pronounced ipso facto by the Œcumeni-

---

[12] Ibidem.
[13] Marucchi: o. c., 70 . . . C. 15 C XII, q. 1.
[14] Ibidem, 83.—*Cod. Just.* Lib. I, Tit, II and III.
[15] Wernz, *Ius. Dec.* T. III, p. 157.
[16] Moulart: *L'Eglise* et *L'Etat,* 561.
[17] C. 1 D. XCIV,—C. E. XIV, 377.
[18] C. 12, X, *de rebus eccl. aliendi vel non,* III, 13.
[19] C. 59, C. XVI, q. 1.

cal Council of Lyons (1274)[20] against laymen who should seize and detain the temporal goods of the Church, and this was virtually repeated by the Fifth Lateran Council[21] and by the Council of Trent.[22]

The principle enunciated in the above legislative enactments is also insisted upon in various doctrinal decrees to which a few references should suffice. John XXII clearly teaches that Christ and the Apostles held true ownership in the goods which they possessed, and that the goods of the Church are not rightfully at the disposition of the Emperor. This teaching is found in two Decrees, "Cum inter non nullos," November 13, 1323, and "Licet juxta doctrinam," October 23, 1323, aimed at Marisglio of Padua and John of Jandun.[23] Again, the teaching of Wyclif and Hus to the effect that it is contrary to the will of Christ and the doctrine of the Sacred Scripture for ecclesiastics to have temporal goods, and that the State can, at will, deprive the Church of her possessions, was condemned by the Council of Constance.[24] During the past century, since the confiscation of Church property has become a common practice, various Popes have become more and more explicit in defining the relation of Church and State in this matter,[25] and Pope Pius IX, in 1864,[26] went so far as to condemn the statement that the claim advanced by civil governments to the ownership of all Church property could be reconciled with the principles of sound theology and canon law.

The Fathers of the Third Plenary Council of Baltimore

---

[20] C. 13, *de electione et electi potestate,* I, 6, in VI°.

[21] Leo X (in Conc. Lat. V) Const. "supernae dispositionis," 5 maii, 1514, par. 39—*Fontes* n. 65.

[22] Sess. XXII, De ref., c. 11.

[23] Denzinger-Bannwart *Enchiridion,* nn. 494, 495.—c. 4, *de verborum significatione,* xiv, extrav. Joann. xxii.

[24] Martin V (in Conc. Constantien.) const. "Inter cunctas," Feb. 22, 1814, art. 10, 16, 32, 33, 36, 39, 44, Ioannis Wicleff damn. art. 34–36 de suibus errorum Wicleff et Hus suspecti interrogandi—*Fontes* n. 43.

[25] Gregorius XVI, allocutio "Afflictas" 1 mart., 1841—*Fontes* n. 496; Pius IX, Allocutio "Quibus Iuctuosissimis" 5 sept. 1851—*Fontes,* n. 512; Allocutio "Nunsuam fore" 15 dec., 1856—*Fontes,* n. 522; Allocutio "Iamdudum cernimus" 18 mart., 1861—*Fontes,* n. 530.

[26] Pius IX, ep. encycl., "Quanta cura" 8 dec. 1864,—*Fontes,* n. 542; Syllabus errorum, prop. 26, 27—*Fontes,* n. 543.

(1884) did not hesitate to apply this long-established principle to the United States,[27] and they expressed regret that "in many parts of the United States the civil laws concerning the possession and administration of temporal goods rest upon principles which the Church cannot admit, without departing from the rule which she has always held from the time when she first became free to put her religious principles into practice."[28]

It is a foregone conclusion that, if the property rights of the Church are established by divine positive law, it is the will of God that they be recognized in the United States. But, because it is impossible under the Federal and State Constitutions of this country[29] legally to recognize any Church as being divinely established, some other basis of recognition should be sought. This other mode of recognition is to be found in what has already been said about the natural right of men to hold property dedicated to religious purposes. In other words, since the United States does not seem to assume in her legislation that there is any divinely established religion, she should apply the principle which would have been applicable in case no special religion had actually been established by God.

But there exists or did exist another basis for recognition, in parts of the United States formerly owned by Catholic nations. The Church, in these sections, held property in accordance with canon law, and it would seem that the United States, in conformity with her own constitution, which prohibits states from impairing the obligation of contracts,[30] should, upon acquiring a given territory, leave the possessions of the Church in statu quo. Baart in this connection says that "When new territory is acquired. the United States government can stipulate by treaty with the foreign power by whom the territory is ceded, that it will respect the title of Church and private property. Moreover, until such territory is properly organized and

[27] Tit. IX, cap. i, n. 264.

[28] Tit. IX, cap. ii, n. 266.

[29] First Amendment to the Constitution of the United States. Practically all the states have a similar provision in their respective constitutions.—See Desmond, *The Church and the Law,* Appendix A.

[30] Art. 1, Section 10, 1.

admitted into the Union as a state, the United States government has full control over it."[31] This was actually done on the occasion of the Louisiana Purchase and of the acquisition of California, and a similar guarantee was given to Spain in connection with Church property in Porto Rico, Cuba, and the Philippines.[32]

Inasmuch as the Church, in the territories referred to, was in possession of certain rights at the time that these territories were acquired by the United States, it is difficult to understand why any treaties should have been necessary, and why the admission of these territories as states should have impaired the rights of the Church in any respect. The Supreme Court of the United States has held, at various times, that grants of land are contracts within the meaning of the Constitution, and in the case of Dartmouth College versus Woodward, a charter given by the British Crown was held to be a contract of the same character.[33] It would therefore seem to be entirely in conformity with the Constitution of the United States to say that the Church, in territories acquired by the United States, should have been given the same independence which she possessed before the acquisition of such territories. There should be no essential difference between the obligations of England to a private corporation and the obligations of Spain or France to the Catholic Church.

A word may now be said about the rights of the Apostolic See, which Canon 1495 places on a par with those of the Universal Church. According to Augustine:[34]

"The term 'Apostolic See' must be understood according to Canon 7 of the Code. However, here it evidently has the special meaning of the primatial See of Saint Peter, and there seems to be a covert allusion to the temporal power of the Pope. To set forth the whole Roman Question, so-called, would require a treatise for itself. Let us emphasize but two points, namely, (1) that the temporal

---

[31] *The Tenure of Catholic Church Property in the United States of America,* 14.

[32] Ibid 1, c.; Zollmann, *American Civil Church Law,* 47.

[33] Kent, *Commentaries,* I, 413–419.

[34] Augustine, *Commentary,* VI, 552, 553—Cfr. Vermeersch-Creusen. *Epitome,* II, 817; Cocchi, *Commentarium, VI,* 332.

dominion of the Pope in its limited sense, i. e., as it actually existed before 1870, cannot be said to be "juris divini" though it may justly be called providential. Providence and divine right are not identical terms, else the Church would have lacked an essential feature for about seven hundred years; (2) that temporal dominion is compatible with spiritual power; the latter as the superior power, may subject to itself a temporal rule or government, but not conversely, because the power of assimilation is wanting in a merely temporal factor.

"The Apostolic See, then, being the Church personified or visibly vested in the Supreme Pontiff, enjoys the right to possess property to the same extent and in the same sense as the Church at large." The right of the Pope in this respect is a consequence of the monarchial constitution of the Church.[35]

The second paragraph of the Canon under discussion refers to individual churches and other moral persons established by ecclesiastical authority:

Canon 1495.

§ 2. "Etiam ecclesiis singularibus aliisque personis moralibus quae ab ecclesiastica auctoritate in iuridicam personam erectate sint, ius est, ad normam sacrorum canonum bona temporalia acquirendi, retinendi et administrandi."

The precise subjects of the rights here referred to will be considered later. It is sufficient here to point out that the apparent purpose of this paragraph is to extend the rights and exemptions claimed for the Universal Church in § 1 to individual churches and other ecclesiastical moral persons. While these moral persons are not established directly by the divine law, the Church can and does permit them to share in the rights that she possesses by divine law.[36] Since these rights exist in the Universal Church, independent of civil authority, the participation in them on the part of individual churches and other moral persons must also be independent of civil authority, but this will be discussed in connection with the treatment of moral persons.

[35] Tanquerey, *Synopsis Theologiae Dogmaticae,* I, 426, . . .

[36] Cf. *Codex*, Can. 99, 100, 1499, § 2.

CHAPTER III.

Personality of the Church in Public Law.

To the Catholic who looks upon the Church as the mystical body of Christ, there is nothing incongruous in considering this mystical body as being endowed with personality.[1] Christ is the head of the Church, we are its members, and the personality of Him who is with us "all days even unto the consummation of the world"[2] may be said to dominate the Church, both in its internal and external activity. Indeed, this fact is so true that one writer, at least, has not hesitated to trace the history of Christ's life in the history of the Church which He has established.[3]

While this fact forms a basis for nothing more than mystical personality, it is, nevertheless, interesting to note that it seems to have influenced mediaeval thought in the development of corporation law.[4]

The legal foundation is to be found in the Codex Iuris Canonici:

Canon 100.

§ 1. "Catholica Ecclesia et Apostolica Sedes moralis personae rationem habent ex ipsa ordinatione divina; ceterae inferiores personae morales in Ecclesia eam sortiuntur sive ex ipso iuris praescripto sive ex speciali competenits Superioris ecclesiastici concessione data per formale decretum ad finem religiosum vel caritativum."

Anyone attempting to study a question where the laws of two heterogeneous societies are involved will find himself beyond his depth, unless he has at least a remote acquaintance with the notion of personality under both systems of law. The philosopher identifies the term person with a

---

[1] I Cor. 12, 27; Eph. i, 22, 23; Eph. 4, 16; Eph. 5, 2, 3.

[2] Matt. 28, 20.

[3] Benson, *Christ in the Church*.

[4] Gierke-Maitland, *Political Theories of the Middle Ages*, pp. XVIII, 22, . . .

rational being[5] (rationalis naturae individua substantia); but if he attempts to extend this definition to the realm of law, he will find that a rational being is not always considered a person. In the law of the Church, for example, a man is not a legal person if he is not baptized;[6] at Roman law, slaves were not persons, but mere chattels.[7]. The philosopher will further find that not every legal person is a rational being. Besides physical persons, the law recognizes persons of its own creation, which, for lack of a generic term, may be called moral, or juristic persons. These juristic persons are known by various names, under various systems of law, and are not always alike in their nature. Society, moral person, institution, corporation, etc., have not always the same meaning, and extreme care must be taken in the use of terms.

In order to understand the meaning of the term, persona moralis, as used in Canon 100, it will be useful first to describe in a very general way, the pattern in Roman law after which modern personae morales are modelled. The ecclesiastical persona moralis will then be discussed, in its relation to property rights of the Church. Finally, attention will be directed to the notion of moral personality as it exists in the law of the United States.

I. MORAL PERSONS IN ROMAN LAW.—Rights are considered by jurists, as well as moralists, to be inherent only in persons; and just as natural rights require a natural

---

[5] Persona, from the Latin "per" meaning through, and "sonare," to sound, was a term originally applied to a mask worn by players on the Latin stage. (Smith: Dictionary of Greek and Roman Antiquities, p. 887.) It would seem that the audience abstracted from the player himself, and identified him with the part that he took in the play or the disguise through which his voice resounded (the persona). At any rate, the term was later applied to the part, which an individual played in the drama of civil life. Thus, just as an actor could in turn play many parts, so an individual among the Romans could, at various times, assume the role of different legal persons, such as creditor, owner, guardian and the like. To do this, however, he had to have capacity under the law in much the same manner as a player must have talent before he is given a part. Person and human being were not equivalent terms. (Sherman, l. c.; Cavagnis: Institutiones Iuris Publici Ecclesiastici, Vol. I, p. 6.) The Philosophical application of the term persona to denote a rational being, was a later development. (Maroto: Institutiones Iuris Canonici, I, 455.)

[6] Canon 87.

[7] Sherman: *Roman Law in the Modern World,* II, 23-26.

person as their subject, so legal rights require legal personality. In Roman law, as in other legal systems, personality was the capacity to possess rights. This capacity, in early times, seems to have been limited to individual human beings. These individuals could unite in various societies (collegia, sodalities, etc.), but property destined for these societies had to be vested in one or more individual members, and belonged not to the society, for it had no personality, but to the members themselves.[8]

This rule, however, did not apply to res publicae, or the common property of the Populus Romanus. Res publicae could not be the object of private ownership. The law looked upon such property as extra commercium.[9] In the domain of private law it was considered res nullius, but in practice the State had full control over it, and the State thus possessed the principal element of personality, though it was, at the time, outside the scope of private law.[10]

Towards the close of the republic, the common property of municipalities, formerly held as res publicae, was brought into the domain of private law, and thus municipalities had, in some respects, the status of private persons. The next step was to consider various lawful societies as having a status akin to that of the municipality, and, in consequence, to endow them with legal personality. Finally, the State itself came to be considered a person, even in private law, although possessing many privileges that testify to its original exemption from the realm of private jurisprudence.[11]

Persons of this character, existing in contemplation of law, are commonly spoken of as juristic or moral persons, as distinct from natural persons.[12] When formed by groups of individuals, as in the cases mentioned above, they are known to modern commentators on Roman law as universitates personarum, or corporations.[13] Modern commentators also speak of another class of persons, formed by col-

---

[8] Sohm-Ledlie: *The Institutes of Roman Law*, 102, . . .

[9] Ibid.

[10] Ibid.

[11] Ibid.

[12] Wernz-Vidal: *Ius Canonicum*, II, 24.

[13] Sohm-Ledlie, o. c., 101; Wernz-Vidal, o. c., II, 25.

lections of goods, and known as universitates bonorum, foundations, or institutions,[14] but it is difficult to support the theory that the sources considered these as having a distinct personality. The idea of attributing moral personality to them seems to have developed at a period later than Justinian's time.

It is not even expressly stated in the Corpus Iuris Civilis that corporations are juristic persons; but their personality can be inferred from the fact that they possessed personal right, such as dominion, action, in court, etc.,[15] and that these rights were distinct from the rights of the individual members.[16]

The Roman State was a moral person,[17] but it differed by its very nature from private corporations; being supreme in its sphere, it did not need the approbation of private law for its existence.[18] It was a perfect society, or what various authors call a persona juridica perfecta,[19] a political corporation,[20] or a public corporation.[21] Other political corporations such as cities, municipalities, etc., were modelled after the State, but depended upon the State as a minor depends on his guardian.[22]

Private corporations had to have some sort of legal recognition.[23] It is not certain that they had to be expressly created by the State; it seems that a purpose which was not prohibited by law was sufficient to give individuals the right to incorporate.[24]

For the formation of a corporation three physical persons were necessary,[25] but, once established, the corporation could continue to exist as long as a single member should

---

14 Sohm-Ledlie, o. c., 101; Wernz-Vidal, o. c., II, 26.

15 *Digest,* Lib. III, Tit. IV, 7, I, Digest, Lib. XL, Tit. III, 1.

16 "Si quid universitati debetur singulis non debetur: nec quod debet universitas, singuli debent." *Digest,* Lib. III, Tit, IV, 7, 1.

17 Sherman, o. c., II, 118; Iulii Pauli *Sent.* 5, 12; *Dig.* 49, 14; *Code* 10, 1.

18 Wernz-Vidal, o. c., 25.

19 Cavagnis is an authority for the use of this term.—*Institutiones Iuris Publici Ecclesiastici,* I, 7.

20 Wernz-Vidal, l. c.

21 Sherman, l. c.

22 Wernz-Vidal, l. c.

23 Ibid.

24 Dig., 47, 22, 3.

25 Dig., 50, 16, 85.

survive.[26] Membership could be changed from time to time and thus the corporation could be considered perpetual.[27]

Since the personality of a corporation was not natural, but juristic, it is evident that it could not function in all respects as a human being. It had to have a will to direct its external acts, and this was provided for in the magister universitatis, through whom the corporations acted as a minor acted through his guardian.[28]

II. Moral Persons in Canon Law.—It was under Roman law that the Church began to function, and it is therefore not remarkable to find that she accepted the Roman notion of moral personality.[29] There are numerous passages in the Corpus Iuris Civilis, attesting the fact that ecclesiastical moral persons were recognized in the law of Justinian,[30] and this recognition was undoubtedly the reason why the Church adopted the convenient legal notion of attributing personality to organizations under her control. To trace the history of this conception through the ages would be outside the scope of this thesis,[31] but it is worth while noting that from ecclesiastical corporations in England, the English idea of corporations evolved.[32] Before the promulgation of the Codex Iuris Canonici, canonists distinguished between real moral persons, the equivalent of Roman corporations, and fictitious moral persons, the equivalent of Roman institutions.[33]

In Canon 100 the Code mentions two distinct kinds of moral persons: (1) the Catholic Church and the Apostolic See, both existing by divine law, (2) other inferior moral persons, existing by ecclesiastical law.[34] The first, being supreme in its sphere, is analogous to the Roman State, the second to inferior Roman corporations.

---

[26] Dig., 3, 4, 7, 2.

[27] Ibid.

[28] Wernz-Vidal, *Ius Canonicum,* II, 25; Dig., 46, 8, 9.

[29] Wernz-Vidal, *Ius Canonicum,* II, 26.

[30] Cfr. *Codex Iust.,* 1, 2, 1; 1, 2, 14, 2; 1, 2, 22.

[31] Gierke-Maitland, o. c. furnishes some excellent material for research on this subject, particularly in the scholarly notes contained in the appendix.

[32] Blackstone,*Commentaries,* I, 469.

[33] Cavagnis, *Institutiones Iuris Publici Ecclesiastici,* I, 7.

[34] "Publica auctoritate constituta"—Canon 99.

It is curious to note that this Canon does not say "Ecclesia Catholica et Apostolica Sedes *sunt* personae morales" (the Catholic Church and the Apostolic See *are* moral persons), but "moralis personae rationem habent" (*have the nature* of moral persons). In Canon 99 we read "In Ecclesia, praeter personas physicas *sunt* etiam personae morales." The "personae morales" of Canon 99 are evidently the "ceterae inferiores personae morales" of Canon 100. Whether or not the Code intends the two expressions "sunt" and "rationem habent" to convey slightly different meanings, the phrasing is happily chosen; for legal personality was, originally, a gift of human law, and, since the Church is divinely established, her personality cannot be given by any human power—it comes from God. While the term persona moralis is now used in reference to perfect, as well as imperfect societies, the slight difference in the wording of the two canons suggests the difference in the constitution of the two categories of personae morales. It will be noted later, that in English and United States law the canonical conception of moral personality does not prevail. The term persona moralis is used in Canon 100 according to its canonical signification; but the word ratio so increases the extension of the first paragraph of this Canon, that the Canon can be applied in any system of law. Moreover, it is possible to conceive of the Church functioning in a country whose system of law does not take cognizance of moral persons, since moral personality is nothing more than a convenient legal fiction, with some foundation in fact. Uncivilized people, for example, can hardly be expected to have developed a legal notion that it took Rome centuries to evolve. Even in such a country the phrasing of Canon 100 would still be intelligible, if taken to mean that the Church and the Apostolic See have, by divine right, all the elements of that legal entity which is known to various systems of law as the persona moralis. Taken in this sense, the first paragraph of Canon 100 is a principle of public law, the embodiment, in legal terminology, of the dogmatic truth that the Catholic Church with the Pope at its head is the divinely established and perfect society of the spiritual order and must be recognized as such throughout the world.

"Ceterae inferiores personae morales eam sortiuntur." "Eam" evidently refers to "rationem." Canon 99 says that there are moral persons in the Church; Canon 100 takes this for granted and seems to give to the moral persons of Canon 99 a share in the "moralis personae rationem" of the Church itself. Interpreted in this way, it would appear that the Code is laying down another principle of public law. These inferior moral persons, although not divinely established, are, nevertheless, here given their rights by a society which is divine. The Church functions through them, and they are not amenable to the civil power.[35] This harmonizes very well with what was said on a previous page in regard to the purpose of Canon 1495, § 2, being to exempt Church property from State control.

The Code follows the Roman law[36] in requiring legal recognition of a persona moralis. The Church itself and the Apostolic See exist by divine law. But inferior moral persons are not recognized as such, unless established by the public authority of the Church.[37] Thus, in Canon 686, § 2, the Ordinary is empowered to approve certain associations; but these associations are not ipso facto moral persons;[38] they become moral persons only when formally erected as such by a legitimate ecclesiastical superior.[39] There are, however, certain juristic entitites such as churches, seminaries, benefices, etc., which the Code itself expressly terms personae morales.[40] These, if properly erected, are ipso facto endowed with legal personality.[41]

Moral persons, according to the Code, are either collegiales or non-collegiales.[42] Personae morales collegiales

---

[35] "Societas imperfecta ad societatem perfectam heterogeniam non per se ipsam comparatur, sed mediante societate perfecta homogenea cuius est pars . . . Solieri, *Institutiones Iuris Ecclesiastici,* 98.

[36] Supra, p. 15.

[37] Canon 99.

[38] Canon 708.

[39] Canon 687.

[40] Canon 99.

[41] Cfr. Canon 1162, . . .

[42] Canon 99.

are modelled after Roman corporations.[43] Three physical persons are required for their establishment,[44] but they continue to exist as long as a single member survives.[45] Personae morales non-collegiales are those which do not consist of physical members; they are either ecclesiastical offices and benefices, or collections of goods destined for some public or charitable purpose, such as divine worship, poor relief, etc.[46]

The Code further follows the Roman law[47] in giving moral persons a legal status equivalent to the status of a minor.[48] Thus, minors are generally represented in court by their parents or guardians,[49] and moral persons by their rectors or administrators,[50] and again both minors and moral persons are sometimes entitled to restitutio in integrum.[51]

A final influence of Roman law can be seen in the fact that personae morales are considered in the Code as being perpetual by nature,[52] although they can be suppressed by legitimate authority or may naturally cease to exist.[53] The authority competent to suppress them is, generally speaking, either the authority by which they were established or some superior authority.[54] When they naturally cease to exist de facto, as where a confraternity disbands or a hospital burns, they still exist de iure for one hundred years, and therefore can be revived without any new decree of erection.[55]

It is this element of perpetuity that renders personae morales convenient subjects of ownership in ecclesiastical property. Theoretically, the Pope could, as Vicar of Christ, hold all property either directly or through the agency of

---

[43] Supra, p. 15, 16.
[45] Canon 100, § 2.
[46] Wernz-Vidal, *Ius Canonicum,* II, 30.
[47] Supra.
[48] Canon 100, § 3.
[49] Canon 1647, § 2
[50] Canon 1649.
[51] Canon 1688, § 1.
[52] Canon 102, § 1.
[53] Ibid.
[54] Cfr. Maroto, *Institutiones Iuris Canonici,* I, 544, . . .
[55] Cfr. Canon 102, § 1. Maroto, l. c.

a physical person.[56] But both of these systems of tenure would manifestly be accompanied by great inconveniences; on the one hand it would be morally impossible for the Holy See, even through a central agency, properly to administer all the temporalities of the Universal Church, and, on the other hand, it would be almost as difficult to readjust these temporalities at the death of the various individuals in whose names they would be vested. The perpetual character of personae morales offers an ideal solution, and the Church has wisely legislated that Church property shall belong to the moral person that legitimately acquires it.[57] Being perpetual by nature, these moral persons can hold property in perpetuum. Being partakers in the divine rights of the Church, they can hold it independent of civil authority. But being dependent for their existence on the authority of the Church, they are amenable to this authority and their rights, in relation to the Church are not absolute.

This is the reason why the same canon that gives them ownership in whatever property they legitimately acquire, places this property under the supreme dominion of the Holy See.[58] As long as they continue to function according to the law by which they were established, their property rights remain. But if they cease to exist their property generally escheats to the Church and vests in the persona moralis immediately superior to them. We say generally, because in individual cases it might be otherwise: the original granter might have stipulated that, in case the persona moralis should become extinct, the property should revert to someone else ;or someone might have a lien on the

[56] While St. Thomas, 2, 2, quest. 100, art. 1, ad septimum says "Res Ecclesiasticae sunt eius (i. e. Papae) ut principalis dispensatoris, non tamen sunt eius ut domini et possessoris," Benedict XIV, ep. Cum encyclicas, 24, maii 1754, n. 4. (Fontes, n. 428) says that it is the common opinion of canonists that the Pope is not only the supreme dispensor of ecclesiastical property, but that he has supreme dominion over it. While stating that he does not wish to settle the controversy, he nevertheless adds: "Concurrente iusta causa, conveniunt omnes tam canonistate quam theologi, Papam, uti supremam administratorem ac dispensatorem bonorum ecclesiasticorum, posse res uni ecclesiae aufferre et dare alteri." It would therefore seem that the Pope could hold at least the legal title to Church property, if he so desired.

[57] Canon 1499, § 2.

[58] Ibid.

the property; or the constitution of the extinct persona moralis might have a clause regulating the disposition of the property. In these and similar cases it is the law of the Church that the rights of others be respected.[59]

III. Moral Persons in the Law of the United States.—The form which the moral person assumed in English and United States law is that of the corporation.[60] Chancellor Kent says:[61] "A corporation is a franchise possessed by one or more individuals, who subsist, as a body politic, under a special denomination, and are vested, by the policy of the law, with the capacity of perpetual succession, and of acting in several respects, however numerous the association may be, as a single individual."

From the fact that the same author[62] defines a franchise as a certain privilege conferred by grant from government, and vested in individuals, it is manifest that corporations, under our system of law, are created by the State. This conclusion is borne out by the fact that in England the King's consent, expressed or implied, was absolutely necessary for the erection of any corporation,[63] and in the United States they are created by the authority of the legislature, and not otherwise.[64] In both England and the United States, it is true, corporations are sometimes deemed to exist by prescription,[65] but only when they have functioned as such, for "time whereof the memory of man runneth not to the contrary," and then because the presumption is that a franchise was originally given.

Corporations in our system of law are aggregate, when consisting of several persons, or sole, when consisting of a single individual.[66] The right to exist as a corporation sole was given in English law to the King, to bishops, deans and the like, in order to prevent their corporate property from falling to their heirs at their death. The corporation

[59] Canon 1501.

[60] Blackstone, *Commentaries,* I, 467, . . . Kent, *Commentaries,* II, 267, . . .

[61] Kent, *Commentaries,* II, 268.

[62] Kent, *Commentaries,* II, 458.

[63] Blackstone, *Commentaries,* I, 472.

[64] Kent, *Commentaries,* II, 276.

[65] Blackstone, *Commentaries,* I, 473—Kent, *Commentaries,* II, 277.

[66] Blackstone, *Commentaries,* I, 469—Kent, *Commentaries,* II, 273.

sole was not subject to death, "for the present incumbent, and his predecessors who lived seven centuries ago, are in law one and the same person, and what was given to the one was given to the other also."[67] From the fact that the predecessor and the successor were the same person in law, as well as from the fact that a deed given to a corporation sole usually had to contain the word "successors" in order to pass the fee,[68] it would appear that a corporation sole differs in theory from what modern Romanists call foundations. Although the corporation sole is one of the legal forms recommended by the Third Plenary Council of Baltimore for the holding of Church property in the United States, this form of corporation, as will be seen later, is not very common in this country.

According to English law, another division of corporations, whether aggregate or sole, is into ecclesiastical and lay.[69] The former were those which were founded for spiritual purposes;[70] Augustine[71] says they are not acknowledged in the United States, while Kent,[72] is of the opinion that they have their counterpart in the so-called religious corporations permitted by the enabling acts of certain state legislatures.[73]

There are various other divisions of corporations in the United States, but they do not affect the subject of this thesis. The point that must be emphasized is that corporations in this country are creatures of the State, and that the establishment of a persona moralis by the authority of the Church does not create a corporation within the meaning of the State laws. In order to be recognized by the State as a corporation, such a persona moralis must incorporate under the enabling act of the State in which it functions. Where such incorporation is impossible, or

[67] Blackstone, *Commentaries*, I, 470.

[68] Kent, *Commentaries*, II, 273.

[69] Blackstone: l. c.

[70] Ibid., note 3.

[71] *Commentary*, II, 2.

[72] *Commentaries*, II, 274.

[73] Augustine is probably considering the common law aspect of English ecclesiastical corporations, while Kent is emphasizing the religious aspect. For a discussion of the forms of religious corporations in this country, see Zollmann, o. c., 38, . . .

where it is undesirable on account of the strictures of the local laws, property vested, according to ecclesiastical law, in the persona moralis, must be held, under the State law, through one or more physical persons. In this latter case, the physical person or persons may be clothed according to the State law with both the legal and equitable title, or they may possess only the legal title, while the equitable titles resides in the members of the Church.

The Fathers of the Third Plenary Council of Baltimore provided for these various contingencies in the following manner:[74]

"In the states in which a civil incorporation of parishes or ecclesiastical bodies, such as accords with Church law, does not exist, the bishop himself will be able to become a corporation-sole before the law to hold and administer the property of the whole diocese; or the property of the diocese by a similar law may be committed to the bishop in trust, that he may hold it in the name of the diocese and administer it according to the wish of the Church; or as a last resource the bishop may hold the temporal goods of the diocese and administer them in his individual name, under that absolute title of law which in English is called a fee simple; in which case let the bishop be always mindful, that, although the full ownership of ecclesiastical property is given him by the civil law, nevertheless according to the admonition of the sacred canons, he is not the owner of it but only the administrator."

For a better understanding of this decree of the Third Plenary Council of Baltimore, it will be necessary first to investigate, in more detail, the general attitude of the States toward the Church. The Canon Law governing the tenure of parochial property will then be discussed; and the dissertation will close with a critique of each of the four arrangements recommended by the Council.

---

[74] Concl. Plenarium Balt. III, Tit. IX, cap. ii, n. 267.—Translation of Baart, o. c., 59, 60.

CHAPTER IV.

Civil Personality of the Church in the United States.

The first amendment to the Constitution of the United States provides that "Congress shall pass no law respecting an establishment of religion or prohibiting the exercise thereof." Article IV, Section 2, of the same document provides that "Citizens of each states shall be entitled to all the privileges and immunities of citizens in the several states." While at first blush these provisions might seem to limit the powers of the various states in religious matters, the United States Supreme Court has decided that Article IV, Section 2, has no reference to the question of religious liberty (16 Wallace, 36). Because, under the tenth amendment, the several states retain "All the powers not delegated to the United States by the Constitution, nor prohibited by it to the states," each state is left free to adopt whatever attitude it may choose toward the subject of religion.[1] While in the early days of the Republic state support was given to certain Protestant sects, all the states today have virtually incorporated the first Federal Constitutional Amendment into their respective constitutions.

All forms of religion stand upon an equal footing in the eyes of American Courts. Consequently, the decisions of the Court regarding the rights of one church are, in similar circumstances, applicable to all churches. The states, being independent of one another, are apt to vary a little in their conception of a religious society, and absolute uniformity is not to be expected; but since the Common Law of England is the basis of our own, and since the Common Law grows out of Court decisions, the Courts of one state are usually guided in their opinion by decisions given in other states.[2]

[1] Desmond: *The Church and the Law,* 17, . . . and Appendix A.

[2] Cfr. Zollmann, *American Civil Church Law,* 198.

"The Catholic Church," says Lew Wallace, Jr.,[3] "is not a body 'having legal capacity to acquire and possess property' (Town of Pawlet v. Clarke, 9 Cranch, U. S. Sup Ct. Rep., 292). Indeed as to much of the property, the law has already been settled by the Supreme Courts of Alabama, California, Texas, and The United States. (Antonio v. Estava, 9 Porter (Ala.), 527; Blair v. Odin, 3 Texas, 288; Nobili v. Redman, 6 Cal.; 225; U. S. v. Ritchie, 17 Howard (U. S.), 524."

By "a body having legal capacity to acquire and possess property" Wallace means a corporation. It has been seen that corporations in the United States are creatures of the law, and possess only such powers as the law is inclined to give them. It is important now to know the attitude of the law towards the Church, disregarding the question of its incorporation.

According to a decision given in New York,[4] "The church consists of an indefinite number of persons, of one or both sexes, who have made a public profession of religion; and who are associated together by a covenant of church fellowship for the purpose of celebrating the sacraments and watching over the spiritual welfare of each other."

In an Alabama decision[5] the church is described as "a voluntary association of its members, united together by a covenant or agreement, for the public worship of God, observing the ordinances of His house, the promotion of the spirituality of its membership, and the spirit of divine truth among others as they understand and teach it. It is purely voluntary and is not corporation or a quasi-corporation."

These two decisions fairly represent the descriptions of a church given by the generality of American Courts. The church is not considered as a single juridical persons but as an association of several natural persons, founded upon a kind of multi-lateral agreement or covenant. The rights of a church are then identified with the aggregate rights of

[3] Outlook, 64: 403.

[4] Baptist Church, Hartford v. Witherell, 3 Paige Ch. (N. Y.) 296.—Lincoln, *The Civil Law and the Church,* p. 107.

[5] Hundley v. Collins, 131, Ala., 234.—Lincoln, l. c.

its members, growing out of contracts they have made, one with another. It seems, however, that this is not a principle of public law.

If this theory were held consistently, and considered by the courts to be a principle of public, as well as private jurisprudence, it would mean that religious authority is not recognized in the law of the United States; but, as a matter of fact, "Courts will not review judgments or acts of the governing authorities of a religious organization with reference to its internal affairs, for the purpose of ascertaining their regularity or accordance with the discipline and usages of such organization. It can make no difference whether the governing authority of a religious denomination is confided to one man or to synod or conference, nor whether the mode of procedure permitted to such a person is in accord with the ordinary course of investigations or trials among laymen. Each religious organization must determine its own policy, and be the judge of its own laws."[6] This is the general attitude taken by the Courts of the United States in question where no property rights are involved. It may be set down as a general rule that all purely spiritual questions, whether of doctrine or discipline, custom or law, are left entirely to the churches themselves, that the Courts will interfere with religious organizations only when questions of property or civil rights are involved, and that even in cases where the Civil Courts assume jurisdiction, the decisions of church judicatories as to their own jurisdiction are of great weight.[7]

This attitude is hardly consistent with the theory that a church is a mere voluntary association, based on contract. It does not seem to clear up the situation to say that "One joining an organized society such as a church having a representative form of government under the supervision and control of judicatories known as church courts, agrees by act of membership to abide by the rules, orders and judgments of such courts properly made, and consents that whatever rights and privileges he may possess as a member shall be controlled by such rules, orders and judgment."[8]

[6] Bonacum v. Harrington, 65 Neb., 831.—Lincoln, o. c., 129.

[7] See cases reviewed by Lincoln, o. c., 133–142.

[8] Hayes v. Manning, 172, S. W. (Mo.), 897 (902).—Lincoln, o. c., 326.

If the relations of a member to the church were merely contractual, Civil Courts, while admitting the binding force of a contract, could at least inquire whether or not the terms of the contract were fulfilled. But even this is not within their jurisdiction.

Various Courts, recognizing this inconsistency, have held that the relations of a member to his church are not contractual. "Church relationship stands upon an altogether higher plane, and church membership is not to be compared to that resulting from connection with mere human associations for profit, pleasure, or culture. The church undertakes to deal with spiritual interests. Admission to its fold is prescribed alone by the church professing to act only upon the word of God."[9]

Zollmamn[10] takes the Courts to task for proposing this doctrine. He says: "The jurisdiction thus conceded to church tribunals is certainly an extraordinary one. It far exceeds in scope the jurisdiction conferred upon Civil Courts, all of whom, from the Supreme Court of the United States, down to the humblest Justice Court, are limited in their jurisdiction by constitutional provisions or statutory enactments. It is much in excess of the jurisdiction exercised by the English ecclesiastical courts, whose powers are limited and who for this purpose are subject to the supervision of the common law courts. It cannot rest on any grant of the State, for Church tribunals are not the instrumentalities or agents of the State in any sense. It cannot rest on the consent of the parties, for it goes beyond that consent. It follows that it must rest on 'a higher plane,' must flow from a supernatural source, must be conferred from on high. The Court therefore at this point leaves the solid ground of law and fact and soars into the higher regions of mystic theology. It unfortunately, however, does not explain how this power is conferred. We are left in the dark as to whether such grant is written in the human heart, or transcribed on tablets of stone, or disclosed to mankind in a revelation."

It is respectfully submitted that we are not so much

---

[9] Nance v. Bushby, 91 Tenn., 303.—Lincoln, o. c., 326.

[10] Zollmann, *American Civil Church Law,* 211.

"in the dark" as Mr. Zollmann would infer. While it is true, as he says in another place,[11] that "the state neither establishes, subsidizes nor supports any religion," it does not necessarily follow that "the decisions rendered by the tribunals of the voluntary associations through which church work is carried on in America are removed from the domain of public law and are not technically judgments which must be respected as such by the courts."[12] The failure of the state to establish, subsidize or support any religion does not prevent the state from recognizing the existence of religion. The State does not establish, subsidize or support foreign governments, yet it cannot be denied that she gives them recognition. The fact that the state will not interference with the internal organization of a church, though it will do this in dealing with other voluntary associations, certainly posits recognition of church authority by our courts; and this recognition can best be explained on the theory that the church is considered by our courts as a juridical person in public law.[13]

It does not alter the case to point to decisions holding that the church is not a corporation. It must be insisted upon that in America the term corporation signifies a creature of the state existing under private law. For the courts to define the church as a corporation would be equivalent to claiming jurisdiction over it, and this they have consistently refused to do. The courts do, however, assume jurisdiction over all questions of property rights, and deem these questions to belong to private law. The church in the eyes of the courts is a spiritual society, and while property can be held for spiritual purposes, which the courts will respect, it must be held by persons, physical or moral, over whom the courts have jurisdiction. Even where a church is incorporated, the corporation has nothing to do with the church represented by it, except that it provides

---

[11] o. c., p. 198.

[12] l. c.

[13] In this connection it is interesting to note the courts may even acknowledge the right of the Church to inquisitorial trials, although this method of procedure is absolutely foreign to the spirit of American law. See Bonacum v. Harrington, 65 Neb., 831, Lincoln, o. c., 230.

for its temporal wants[14] and the distinction between the church and the corporation is always outstanding.[15]

Mr. Zollmann[16] is of the opinion that "No one, lawyer or layman, can emerge from an attentive reading of all the cases on this subject but with a mind scratched and bleeding and utterly bewildered by the judicial vagaries encountered." Nevertheless, he attempts to construct a theory on this subject, which may be summed up as follows:[17]

Church relationship in America is based on contract. A person joining a church covenants to abide by its decisions, the stipulations of the covenant being found in the canons, constitutions, articles and by-laws of the chruch, together with the customs and usages which have grown up in connection with these instruments. Some sort of discipline is necessary in the organization, and this, together with promised submission to properly constituted church tribunals, is part of the original agreement. These tribunals are limited by the terms of such agreement and must proceed as therein specified; their right to adjudicate is based solely upon the consent of those who submit their difficulties to them; they may be compared to an architect who, by the consent of the owners and building contractors, is empowered to settle questions in connection with the erection of the building. The result reached by such a tribunal is what it is, not because there is anything sacred about it or because it is better versed in ecclesiastical lore than civil courts, but because of the aforesaid agreement. Its powers are not derived from a supernatural source but spring directly from the contract of those who come before it.

With due respect to the scholarship of Mr. Zollman, the theory that he proposes is exactly what the courts have attempted to avoid. It leads to a species of Caesarism which, while not establishing a definite religion, certainly interferes with the exercise of all religion. Religious freedom would be impossible if the courts were to adopt this

[14] Hardin v. Baptist Church, 51 Mich., 137; 16 N. W., 311.
[15] Gray v. Good, 89 N. E., 498.
[16] o. c., 222.
[17] o. c., 223, . . .

view. It is useless to attempt to construct theories where the courts have refused to do so. The purpose of the law should be to promote justice even at the expense of theory, and it is far better for the courts to leave the matter of church relationship unsettled, by basing it on a higher plane, than to adopt a consistent theory which would give them the same jurisdiction over all church matters that they assume over ecclesiastical property. If consistency is demanded, it should be sought in the other direction; the courts should declare that the property rights of the Church are based on "a higher plane" and are not within the province of private law.

To sum up the present chapter. Citizens of the United States are guaranteed religious freedom by the Federal and State Constitutions, and all religious societies are equal before the law. These societies, including the Catholic Church, are not corporations having civil rights. Although the courts describe them as voluntary associations growing out of common contracts among the members, these same courts, in matters not involving civil rights, assert that church relationship is not founded on contract, but on "a higher plane," which they do not attempt to define. In the absence of any theory regarding this higher plane, it is submitted that there is implied recognition of the personality of the Church in public law. It now remains to be seen how the Church, having no civil personality, is nevertheless enabled to enjoy certain property rights.

CHAPTER V.

Civil Rights of the Church in the United States.

The right of property, as has been seen, is considered by the courts of the United States as pertaining exclusively to the realm of private law. Since this private law does not recognize the personality of the church as such, it follows that the church cannot hold property directly, unless she becomes a private corporation, subject to the laws of the state in which she incorporates. Where this is done the church is said to consist of two elements: (1) the ecclesiastical body, which undergoes no change by the fact of incorporation; (2) the corporation, a creature of the law, which has relation only to the temporalities of the institution. In this case, it is not the church as a spiritual society, but the corporation, as a person in private law, that holds the property. Where no incorporation takes place, some physical person or group of persons must hold the title.

The owner of property under the law can, subject to certain legal limitations, dispose of the property as he sees fit. He may be bound in conscience to use it for church purposes, but the maxim "De internis non iudicat praetor" applies to civil as well as to ecclesiastical law. There must be some juridical act or fact tending to show that the rights are limited, before the courts will recognize any such limitation. The evidence of this limitation of the apparent owner's rights must be of such a nature as to be admissible under the rules of the civil courts. Thus, we can conceive of two possible situations, that may arise either in the case of a physical person or in the case of a corporation: (1) The person holding the property, though bound in conscience to dispose of it subject to the laws of the church, may legally convert it to his own use and leave the church without any redress in the civil courts; (2) he may hold the property in trust or for the use of the church (i. e., the members of the church or some religious purpose), and if this use or trust can be proved under the rules of the court, he will be held responsible by the court to see that the use or trust is carried out. Technically, in the first case he has both the legal and the equitable title, while in the second case he has only the legal title, the equitable title residing in the *cestui qui trust* or the person or persons for whose benefit he holds the property.

It is only where property is held in trust that we can speak of the civil rights of the church, and even then it would be more accurate to speak of the rights of church members. These rights have their origin in the acts and circumstances under which the present owner acquires title. The former owner had the right to dispose of his property as he saw fit. He gave it or sold it to the present owners with the stipulation that it be used for religious purposes. The present owner's rights are limited by the intentions of the former owner, and the persons who would benefit by the religious purposes contained in this intention can go into a court of equity and compel the present owners to carry out the above intention. Again, the present owner might have purchased the property with funds that he held in trust or with funds that he had wrongfully converted; in this case the courts might hold that there is a constructive trust or a resulting trust, as the case may be.

This attitude of the courts towards trusts, while it cannot be said technically to confer any rights upon the church, effects the same thing in a practical manner by interpreting the purpose of the trust according to the doctrine and tenets of the church. It is this fact alone that explains how the church, which under the law has no personality, is nevertheless able to enjoy so many advantages in respect to property. Thus "when property has been acquired, whether by gift or purchase, for the maintenance and support of the faith of any recognized denomination or church, every member of the association acquiring it, corporate or unincorporated, has a right to resist its diversion to other antagonistic uses, whether secular or religious, and therefore those who hold the title or control, whether a corporation, or the officers of the association, hold it charged with a trust to apply to the uses for which it was acquired, and not to inconsistent ones."[1]

"The title to the church property of a divided congregation is in that part of it which is acting in harmony with its own law; and the ecclesiastical laws, usages, customs, and principles which were accepted among them before the dispute began are the standard for determining which party is right."[2]

It makes little difference how many of the congregation agree to divert the trust. "A minority have the right to insist upon carrying out the proposition for which the church or society was organized, and the majority will not be permitted to divert the common property to other uses, or to use it for the support and maintenance of doctrines or a polity essentially at variance with its original constitution."[3]

Even where a congregation becomes schismatic, the same rule applies. "Where a congregation has been organized and holds its property as a constituent part of any particular religious denomination or in subordination to the government of any particular church, it cannot, without just cause, sever itself from such connection or government. If it does so it necessarily forfeits its rights and property to those of the organization who maintain the original status."[4]

---

[1] Marien v. Evangelical Creed Congregation, Milwaukee, 132 Wis., 650.—Lincoln, o. c., 525, 526.

[2] McGinnis v. Watson, 41 Pa. St., 9.—Lincoln, o. c., pp. 526, 527.

[3] Schradi v. Dornfeld, 52 Minn. 465.—Lincoln o. c., 524, 525.

[4] McAuley's Appeal, 77 Pa., 397.—Lincoln o. c., 524.

CHAPTER VI.

Subject of Ownership Under Church Law.

The object of the present chapter will be to set forth some of the rules of law concerning the tenure of property within the organization of the church itself. It is obvious that this question must be touched upon if one is to understand the relative merits of various modes of tenure under the civil law. The main points to be considered are two: (1) In what precise person is the dominion of church property vested? (2) What are the general norms governing the exercise of this dominion?

I. Subject of Dominion.—While the property rights of individual churches, as against the civil power, have long been well defined, much vagueness and diversity of opinion existed, before the promulgation of the Code, as to the precise subjects in which these rights were vested. Vering[1] says that the question is of no practical importance, and that, in consequence, the law, though providing in exact terms for the use and administration of ecclesiastical goods, has made no direct pronouncement regarding their ownership. Although this opinion might have had some weight in former times, the fact is that the Code[2] has undertaken to decide the question of ownership; and a glance at the various theories formerly in vogue will bring out some considerations that will aid in the understanding of the present law.

The theories that will be here considered as having the most importance in the light of the present law, may be called, for want of better names, the theory of supernatural dominion, the theory of papal dominion, and the theory of institutional dominion.[3]

[1] *Droit Canon,* II, 526.

[2] Canon 1499, § 2.

[3] DD. in tit. de Peculio Cleric. (X, iii, 25).—Aichner, Compendium Iuris Canonici, p. 763, seqq.—Carriere: De Iustitia et Iure, I, 164, . . . Ferreres: Institutiones Canonicae, II, 473.—Prummer: Manuale Iuris Ecclesiastici, 443.—Tanquerey: Synopsis Theol. Moralis, II, 85.—Wernz: Ius Dec., III, tit. V.

Theory of Supernatural Dominion.—According to this theory, ecclesiastical goods are under the proximate and immediate dominion of God, not in any metaphorical sense, but in the strict legal sense, so that the members of the Church have nothing more than a kind of franchise to use them. This was the common opinion of Catholic doctors up to the time of Navarrus, who considered it "Irrefragibiliter tenendum,"[4] and it receives greater weight from the fact that Suarez[5] considers it highly probable.

In support of this opinion it might be alleged: (1) That the Old Testament unmistakably asserts that all the tithes of the land are the Lord's and that the first-born of man and beast belong to Him.[6] (2) That the offerings of the faithful are actually made to God, and, therefore, belong to Him by natural right, as property would belong to any other donee.[7] (3) That the sacred canons clearly speak of the goods of the Church as res dominicae, res Deo sacrae, res Dei,[8] pecunias Christi[9] etc., while those who unjustly deprive the Church of her possessions are guilty of sacrilege.[10] (4) That some of the gods owned property in ancient Rome[11] and that Justinian consequently made provision for property left to Jesus Christ, or to an archangel or martyr.[12] (5) That even in England, where the Roman law was not systematically adopted, supernatural dominion over Church property was, nevertheless, recognized.[13] (6) That the supreme test of dominion is the power to alienate property at will, and that not even the Pope can alienate Church property without just cause.[14]

While this theory is not without some foundation, in

[4] *Tr. de Reditibus Ecclesiasticis,* quest. 1, monito 40, Opera Omnia, Tom. II, p. 515 seqq.

[5] *Opera Omnia,* Tom. 24, p. 443, 7.

[6] Lev. 27, 30; Num. 3, 13.

[7] Navarrus, l. c. 13.

[8] c. 21, C 2, q. 1.—Trid. Sess. 25, de ref.

[9] c. 6, C 12, q. 2.

[10] Ibid.—c. 8 & 10, C 12, q. 2.

[11] Ulpian: Frag. 22, 6.

[12] C. 1, 2, 25.

[13] "Most of the clerical and monastic possessions were soon discharged from every servile and unnecessary obligation. By a transition easy to the human mind, they were considered as the property not of man, but of God." Linguard, *Antiquities of the Anglo-Saxon Church,* 80.

[14] Navarrus, l. c., 6 and 10; Suarez, l. c.

law and in fact, the evidence is too vague and indefinite to establish a legal personality in which property rights are vested under the law of the Church. It might have been a principle of the civil law, a crude but picturesque method of removing ecclesiastical property from the jurisdiction of the civil courts. If the civil courts held to this principle, anyone attempting, by process of law, to gain control over ecclesiastical property would have to resort to the ridiculous expedient of bringing suit against God or a saint and the courts would have to dismiss the suit, either for lack of jurisdiction, or because they could not get service on the defendant.[15] But to accept the theory as a principle of canon law, would be to remove Church property from all human control, since no one can have any rights against God. It cannot be denied that God owns the property of the Church, but, by the same token, He also owns the property of the State; and the question as Aichner[16] suggests is not whether God has supreme dominion over the earth, but who, under human law, is to be considered the owner of various kinds of property. It must be added, however, that property once brought under the control of the Church acquires a sacred character[17] and, generally speaking, can never again be converted to profane use.[18] In this sense God may be considered metaphorically as the owner; for the dominion of men over ecclesiastical property is never as perfect as dominion over secular property.

Theory of Papal Dominion.—The proponents of this theory assert that the Pope has supreme dominion over ecclesiastical goods.[19] They argue from the supreme power

[15] This would have been no obstacle to the genius of some of the reformers, if one can give credence to an incident recorded by Lingard (A History of England, Vol. VI, p. 275, 276). On April 24, 1538, Henry VIII, as the story goes, cited St. Thomas a Becket (dead over three hundred years) to appear in court on a charge of high treason. Thirty days elapsed and the saint refused to leave his tomb; whereupon Henry, having assigned him a counsel, found him guilty, confiscated his property and desecrated his bones.

[16] o. c., p. 764.

[17] Cfr. Supra, notes 8, 9, and 10.—Ferrari, *Summa Institutionum Canonicarum,* II, 274.

[18] Ferrari, *Summa Institutionum Canonicarum,* Vol. II, p. 358 seqq.

[19] See Fagnanus: In lib. III Decret. cap. Relatum, *ne clerici vel monachi,* n. 26 seqq.

inherent in the Pope as the head of the Church, and they point to certain expressions used in the old canons which would seem to indicate papal ownership of the entire Church.[20] They further adduce many instances where the popes have administered property as if it were their own.[21]

This theory, like the preceding one, is not so easily ruled out of court. When one considers that under the Feudal System all the land was holden of the king and that the king's vassals were mere tenants who had no dominion as against the crown,[22] it is not difficult to conceive that the Church could have adopted a similar system and considered ecclesiastical persons as tenants of the Pope. The Pope *in foro externo* is beyond all law, and no one can sit in judgment on his official acts.[23] If he were to declare himself the direct owner of all church property it seems that his act would be valid; whether it would be licit is a matter for theologians to determine. The question is whether de facto the Pope has even done this and the arguments adduced by the proponents of this opinion are not conclusive; they can be explained by the doctrine of Saint Thomas[24] that the Pope is the "principalis dispensator."

Theory of Institutional Dominion.—This theory is that the particular dominion over ecclesiastical goods is in particular churches and other canonically erected moral persons as long as they remain united to the universal church, and that the Pope possesses the right of eminent domain,[25] while the bishop of the particular church has the right of supervising the administration of the property. It is the theory that seems to have been favored by the majority of the more recent writers, and has the merit of being the most satisfactory theory for reconciling what seems to be discrepancies in the canonical legislation of the past. This theory has been incorporated into the recent legislation of the Church.

---

20 c 2, D. 19; c 1, D. 22; c 1, D. 97.

21 Fagnanus, l. c.

22 Blackstone, *Commentaries*, II, 60.

23 Canon 1556.

24 *Summa*, 2, 2, quest. 100, art. 1, ad 7.

25 i. e. dominium altum.

Canon 1499.

§ 2. Dominium boronum sub suprema auctoritate Sedis Apostolicae, ad eam pertinet moralem personam quae eadem bona legitime acquisiverit.

Dominium.[26]—This signifies the legitimate power freely to dispose of an object as one's own unless prohibited by superior authority. The free disposition of an object includes the right to possess, to use, to barter, to give away or to destroy; but this right may be limited by superior authority as where the law protects minors by making their contracts voidable; it may also be conditioned by the person who confers the dominion, as where the grantor in a deed stipulates that the property must never be used as a tavern.

It is customary to speak of dominium altum (eminent domain) or the power inherent in public authority to make property laws for the public good, and dominium humile or the dominion of private persons over their own goods; but as Noldin points out, dominium altum is not dominion in the true sense—it is a right of jurisdiction rather than a property right.

Dominion in the true sense is said to be perfect when the person in whom it resides has the right both to the possession and use of the substance, together with full rights to the natural increase of the same. But if the right to use the thing, to possess it for a time, or to receive the increase of it resides in a second person, the dominion is imperfect. The first person then has direct or radical dominion, the second indirect dominion. This indirect dominion may be concerned with the use of the thing, in which case the second person is called the usuarius, or it may be concerned with the right to reap the fruits of the thing, and the second person is then called the usufructuarius.

Bonorum.—The bona to which this canon refers are bona temporalia. This is evident from the caption under which canon 1495 is placed: "Pars Sexta De Bonis Ecclesiae Temporalibus." All kinds of goods are included in this term, whether belonging to the Universal Church, the

[26] Ferraris, *Bibliotheca Prompta*, v. dominium, art. I.—Noldin, *Summa Theologiae Moralis*, II, 357, . . .

Apostolic See, or any other ecclesiastical moral person.[27] Such property is considered to be either corporeal or incorporeal, depending on whether it can, or cannot be perceived by the senses. Thus, bonds, books, vessels, and the like are corporeal, while actions, rights, obligations, etc., are incorporeal. Corporeal property is considered sacred, when dedicated to divine service by being consecrated or blessed, as are altars, chalices, oratories, etc.; it is further said to be precious when it is of considerable value, owing to the material of which it is composed, or the artistic skill with which it is wrought, or the historical associations which cluster around it.[28]

Sub Suprema Auctoritate Sedis Apostolicae.—This supreme authority, according to commentators, means dominium altum, or eminent domain. It is a right of jurisdiction, in virtue of which the Pope can, for a sufficient reason, limit the property rights of ecclesiastical entities.[29]

Ad Eam Pertinet Moralem Personam Quae Eadem Bona Legitime Acquisiverit.—This is the decisive phrase of the present canon. As Vermeersch-Creusen[30] point out, it partly repudiates the theories mentioned at the beginning of this chapter. Ecclesiastical goods are not vested exclusively in God, nor in the Pope, nor in the Universal Church, but there are as many subjects of dominion as there are personae morales in the Church.[31] According to some canonists,[32] the reason for this is the incongruity of positing ownership in God or in the Pope; for God or the Pope would, in this case, be responsible for all the debts of the Church. Carriere[33] gives a still better reason. "It is sufficiently patent," he says, "from the will of the donors." Nearly all church holdings, or, at least, the funds used to purchase them, are acquired by gifts devises and bequests

[27] Canon 1497, § 1.—Cocchi: *Commentarium,* VI, 334.

[28] Canon 1497, § 1.—Cocchi, l. c.—What value an article must have to be considered precious, is a controverted question. See authorities in Cocchi, l. c.

[29] Cocchi, o. c., Vol. VI, p. 347.—Vermeersch-Creusen, o. c., Tom. II, p. 467.—Prummer, o. c., Q. 443.

[30] *Epitome,* Tom. II, p. 467.

[31] Ibid.

[32] Wernz, o. c., Tom. III, 199.—Prummer, o. c., Q. 443.

[33] o. c., 173.

of the faithful. Though the faithful look upon donations made to the Church as offerings made to God, they likewise have in mind the particular cause for which the offering is requested. This can readily be seen by comparing the amounts given in two collections taken up on the same day, one for the parish, which is deeply in debt, and the other for an outside charity.

Perhaps no commentator on the present law has explained this point more clearly than did Carriere long before the promulgation of the Code. A free translation of his statement of the case is submitted:[34]

"1° Church property in France, as an example, does not belong to the Church in general; for it is evident that the churches of other countries, v. g. Italy, Spain, etc., have no claim upon the property.. 2° Such property does not even belong to the Church in France, or the French clergy; the church at Lyons, for example, cannot claim property situated in the ecclesiastical province of Paris. The French clergy did, at one time, form a corporation representing various particular churches; but because this corporation exercised certain acts of administration over the property of the churches, it does not follow that the corporation owned the property. 3° Church property situated in a certain diocese does not belong to the diocese in general. Various churches in the same diocese can have their own individual property; the same can be said of various societies or communities, like the former religious communities[35] which certainly had dominion over their particular property. Church property must therefore be said to belong to the particular moral persons that acquired them by gift or by some other just title."

The foot-notes under this canon refer the reader to other parts of the Code, where examples are to be found of various religious institutions, pious foundations, etc., capable of possessing property. With these we are not concerned, as they have no direct bearing on the tenure of parochial property. The particular question that must be examined at this point, is, who owns the property of a parish? Cer-

[34] Carriere, l. c.

[35] This was written in France in 1839.

tainly the parochial persona moralis that legitimately acquires it. But is this the parochial community as a persona moralis collegialis, or is it, in every case a persona moralis non-collegialis?

In other words, is the juristic entity which canon law clothes with the title to parochial property, an entity composed of the members of the parish as a corporation (universitas personarum), or is it a collection of goods equivalent to the Roman institution (universitas bonorum), to which the law fictitiously attributes personality?

Canonists seem to agree that the parochial community does not own the property of the parish, but their reasons, where reasons are given, do not seem to be compelling.

Wernz,[36] writing before the promulgation of the Code, denied dominion in the parochial community on the ground that the parochial community has no control over the property. As Vermeersch-Creusen[37] point out, one could as well apply the same argument to the Universal Church. It must be confessed that a persona moralis generally acts, not through the individuals composing it, but through its rector or administrator. Therefore, the fact that the parochial community has no voice in the administration of the property is not ad rem.

Vermeersch-Creusen, though critical about the reasoning of Wernz, are inclined to agree with his opinion. The reason they give for this opinion is, that the parochial community is *not erected* as a persona moralis. Had they declared outright that the parochial community *is not* a persona moralis, this, reason, if true, would be conclusive; for according to Canon 1495 dominion over Church property must be vested in a persona moralis. But it is one thing to say that the parochial community *is not erected* as a persona moralis; it is an entirely different thing to say that it *is not* a persona moralis. Strictly speaking, a persona moralis need not be erected as such, but may receive its personality "ex ipso iuris praescripto,"[38] and this prescription, as Maroto[39] points out, need not be stated in

[36] *Ius. Dec.* II, 139.
[37] *Epitome*, II, 467.
[38] Canon 100, § 1.
[39] *Institutiones Iuris Canonici*, I, 534.

express terms, but may be implied by law. According to Chelodi,[40] it is implied when a certain entity is considered in law as being capable of possessing rights. Granted that the parochial community is not erected as a persona moralis, is its personality nevertheless express or implied by the Code? There are some indications that it is,[41] but these indications are not conclusive, and the question may be dismissed, since it has only a negative bearing on the point at issue: moral personality would make the parochial community capable of possessing dominion, but would not, ipso facto, confer dominion upon it; the absence of such personality, however, would render the community incapable of possessing dominion.

According to the commentators, the subject of dominion over parochial property is the parish church, the sacred edifice itself, considered in law as if it were a person—"Ipsae aedes sacrae" (Blat, Cocchi)—"Singulae institutiones [Recall the difference between institutio and corporatio.] quae in ens iuridicum ab Ecclesia erectae sunt" (Cocchi)—"Ecclesiae paroeciales" (Vermeersch-Creusen)—"Penes ipsa loca pia" (Bargilliat)[42]. This opinion seems to be well founded. Canon 1495, § 2, declares that individual churches and other moral persons (ecclesiis singularibus, aliisque personis moralibus) have certain property rights. There is good reason for believing that the term ecclesia, in this connection, should be interpreted according to Canon 1161, as a sacred edifice; it is true that in the canons immediately following Canon 1498 the term ecclesia may signify any persona moralis, but to apply Canon 1498

---

[40] *Ius de Personis,* 161, note 3.

[41] Canon 2255, 3, e.g., speaks of suspension and interdict affecting a community as a persona moralis, and from the nature of the case it would seem that parochial communities are included. In Canon 1653, 2, all holders of benefices (including pastors) are given the right to represent their benefices in court, but to do this licitly they are required to obtain permission as prescribed in Canon 1526; if they act illicitly in this matter, the community, or the pia causa, as the case may be, has a right to indemnity (4 of Canon 1653); 2 certainly includes pastors, but it is a question whether the word communitas in § 4 includes the parochial community.

[42] Blat, *Commentarium Textus Codicis Iuris Canonici,* III, 489.—Cocchi, *Commentarium,* VI, 333, 347.—Vermeersch-Creusen, *Epitome,* II, 467.—Bargilliat, *Praelectiones Iuris Canonici,* II, 379.

in the interpretation of Canon 1495 would lead to the ridiculous paraphrase: "Etiam cuidam personae morali aliisque personis moralibus, etc." Moreover, a church is mentioned in Canon 99 as a persona moralis non-collegialis, and there seems to be no doubt that the Code here appropriates the Roman notion of an institution (universitas bonorum), and speaks of a thing as if it were a person. Thus, instead of declaring that the Church of St. Rose belongs to God, or to St. Rose, or to the Pope, the law declares that this church is itself a person, and holds its own property. "The church (subject) owns the church (object)," . . . "As a garden belongs to a house, as a stopper belongs to a bottle, not as a house and bottle belong to a man."[43]

It does not seem definitely established, however, that the parochial church owns all the property of a parish. A parish, according to Canon 216, is a part of a diocese (usually a territorial part), with its own church, its own rector, and a determined group of people. It is spoken of as being "constituted"[44] or "erected,"[45] and these terms seem to indicate that it has the status of a persona moralis.[46] It also seems, from Canon 1415, that as a persona moralis the parish is identical with the parochial benefice; if this were not the case, there would be no reason for exempting parishes in § 3 of this canon from the rule laid down in § 1 concerning benefices. Now, the benefice must have a dowry (dos), and this dowry according to Canon 1410 may sometimes consist of an endowment, the ownership of which is vested in the juridical entity itself (bona quorum proprietas est penes ipsum ens iuridicum). According to some commentators, the term juridical entity (ens iuridicum) in this canon refers to the benefice; if this is true, there are at least two subjects of dominion in the parish, scil., the parochial church, and the parochial benefice. Again, the dowry may consist merely of offerings due from a certain family or from a certain persona moralis, certain

[43] Maitland, *The Corporation Sole,* The Law Quarterly Review, XVI, 335.

[44] Canon 216, § 4.

[45] Canon 1415.

[46] Cir. Maroto, *Institutiones Iuris Canonici,* I, 542.

offerings of the faithful, etc., and in this case the law does not state that the property, though comprising the dowry, belongs to the juridical entity. Canon 1409 states that one element of a benfice is the right to receive an income from the dowry, but it does not state that ownership of the dowry is vested in the benefice. It is ventured that the commentators may have erred in interpreting the term "ens iuridicum," in Canon 1410, as meaning the benefice itself: there is a possibility that the term refers to "dotem," rather than to "beneficii," and that the dowry is considered by the law as a pia causa, or a persona moralis in itself;[48] there is also a possibility that the term refers to the parochial church to which the benefice is attached;—certainly the parochial church is an ens iuridicum, and since the parish is an organized unit, it would be convenient to have all its property vested in a single persona moralis.

Whether all the property of a parish belongs to the parochial church, or whether it belongs partly to the church, partly to the benefice, and partly to one or more piae causae, it is, in every case, removed from the dominion of human beings, and placed under the dominion of a persona moralis non-collegialis which partakes of the divine rights of the Universal Church. The one point that the Code has settled is, that individual parishes have individual rights. If the property of St. John's Church belonged to God, or to the Pope, or to the Universal Church, it would not constitute alienation to use this property for some other religious purpose, since the dominion over the property would remain unchanged. Now, however, such conversion would be tantamount to depriving St. John's Church of its dominion, and would seem to require the exercise of eminent domain, which the Pope alone possesses.

II. Exercise of Dominion.—Since the owner of parochial property is a persona moralis, it is manifest that this person must act through one or more administrators. To give a detailed explanation of the canons governing the administration of this property would require a separate thesis. Nevertheless, it is necessary to refer to some of

---

[48] Cfr. Canon 1653, where the term "pia causa" in § 4 refers to the term "beneficium" in § 2.

them in a general way, in order to have a criterion by which various modes of civil tenure can be judged. In doing this it may be useful to consider four classes of persons who, according to the canons, may be involved in the administration of parish property, scil., the Pope, the ordinary, the pastor, and the laity.

(*a*) *The Pope.*—In addition to placing dominion over church property under the supreme authority of the Holy See,[49] the Code declares that the Roman Pontiff is the supreme administrator and dispensor of all ecclesiastical goods.[50] This is a necessary corollary to the fact that all inferior moral persons in the Church are mere participants in the personality of the Church Universal.[51] Since the Roman Pontiff has supreme jurisdiction over the Church as a whole, his jurisdiction over every part of it must likewise be supreme. Inferior administrators of personae morales are therefore his agents, and he subjects them to constant vigilance in the exercise of their office, while he reserves certain important matters to himself.[52]

The chief matters which the Holy See reserves to itself are: (1) the alienation, or the perpetual transfer to another church, of relics which are considered extraordinary (insignes), of precious images, or of other relics or images that are the object of special veneration by the people in a particular church[53]; (2) the alienation of things regarded as precious, or of property exceeding thirty thousand francs in value.[54] Attempted alienation of these objects without the permission of the Holy See is invalid,[55] and anyone guilty of such attempt incurs non-reserved excommunication latae sententiae, besides being bound to restitution.[56]

---

49 Canon 1499, § 2.

50 Canon 1518.—St. Thomas 2-2, Q. 100, art. 1 ad 7; Benedict XIV ep. cum encyclicas, 24 maii 1754 n. 4 (Fontes n. 428).

51 Canon 100.

52 Cocchi, *Commentarium,* VI, 386.

53 Canon 1281.

54 Canons 1530, 1532. The alienation of votive offerings requires the permission of the Holy See, and all offerings made at an altar, or sacred image are presumed to be votive offerings.—AAS, XI, 416–419.—AAS XIV, 160–161.

55 Canons 1281, 1530.

56 Canon 2347.

(*b*) *The Ordinary.*—The function of the local ordinary in the administration of parochial property is given in Canon 1519; but the exact meaning of this canon will probably remain uncertain until an authentic interpretation is handed down.

Canon 1519.

§ 1. Loci ordinarii est sedulo advigilare administrationi omnium bonorum ecclesiasticorum quae in suo territorio sint nec ex eius iurisdictione fuerint subducta, salvis legitimis praescriptionibus, quae eidem potiora iura tribuant.

§ 2. Habita ratione iurium, legitimarum consuetudinum et circumstantiarum, Ordinarii, opportune editis peculiaribus instructionibus intra fines iuris communis universum administrationibus bonorum ecclesiasticorum negotium ordinandi curent.

The first part of paragraph one is clear enough. The local ordinary has the right and the duty to keep strict watch over the administration of all ecclesiastical property located in his diocese and not exempt from his jurisdiction. But what is meant by the qualifying clause "salvis legitimis praescriptionibus, quae eidem potiora iura tribuant"?

Woywod[57] paraphrases this clause as follows:

"He [the Ordinary] may, however, have acquired jurisdiction even over exempt goods by prescription."

It does not seem that this clause refers merely to exempt goods; the punctuation seems to demand that it qualify the entire paragraph. Moreover, if the ordinary has no right over exempt property in the first place, it is incongruous for the Code to speak of him acquiring greater rights (potiora iura).

Cocchi[58] interprets this clause in an entirely different way:

"Salvis legitimis praescriptionibus (contentis in tabulis fundationis vel privilegiis) quam eisdem (Ordinariis) potiora iura (quam solum ius vigilantiae) tribuant."

It is submitted that Cocchi's paraphrase is the preferable one. It seems, however, that the term "praescription-

[57] *The New Canon Law,* p. 306.

[58] *Commentarium,* VI, 386, 387.—Blat, *Commentarium,* III, 528.

ibus" should be given a somewhat broader interpretation. It is suggested that this term may be intended to include not only special provisions of a foundation and special privileges, but also special prescriptions in the Code itself, where the Ordinary is certainly given more than the right of watching over the administration of property—for example, in the matter of dividing parishes.[59]

The second paragraph of this canon instructs the Ordinary to regulate the entire matter of the administration of goods in his diocese, with due regard to the rights of individuals, to legitimate customs and to special circumstances of time or place. This should be done by diocesan statutes[60] binding the entire diocese, but keeping within the limits of the common law.

The question whether the local Ordinary is the supreme administrator of non-exempt ecclesiastical goods in his own territory is controverted by the commentators. The reason for the controversy seems to lie in the fact that the Code speaks of the pastor being the administrator of certain parochial property,[61] and the Pope being the supreme administrator of all ecclesiastical property[62] while the province of the Ordinary is to watch over the administration.[63]

Augustine[64] asserts that the bishop has the "intentio fundata in iure," that is, "the original right of administering all diocesan property because he is the pastor of the whole territory." Blat[65] says that the Code presupposes this right, and therefore modifies it; he argues from the modus loquendi of Canon 1520, and from a decision of the Propaganda which held that the bishop had the right of administration "ad formam canonum et iuxta intentionum fundatorum" while the priests had such right "sub dependentia Episcopi"[66] Vermeersch-Creusen,[67] however, assert that the bishop has only the right of supervision and regu-

[59] Canon 1427.

[60] Augustine, *Commentary,* VI, 579.

[61] Canon 1182.

[62] Canon 1518.

[63] Canon 1519.

[64] *Commentary*, VI, 578.

[65] *Commentarium,* Liber III, n. 434.

[66] Collect, S. Congr. de Prop. Fide, 1 Aprilis, 1816 (C. G.) n. 712, ad 2 and 4.

[67] *Epitome,* II, 481.

lation; that it is against the policy of the law, which establishes distinct benefices, for the bishop to administer these benefices himself; that such an act would be not only illicit but invalid.

The Code reserves to the local Ordinary the matter of alienating ecclesiastical goods in all cases not reserved to the Holy See, and consent of the Ordinary in this matter is necessary for the validity of the act.[68] Where the property in question is worth more than one thousand francs, the consent of the chapter, the board of administrators, and those interested must also be obtained.[69] If the value of the property does not exceed one thousand francs, it suffices that the board of administrators be consulted, although the consent of those who have a special interest in the property is still necessary.[70] Where these formalities are not complied with, the act of alienation is invalid.[71]

Another function of the local Ordinary is to regulate the distribution of the revenues of a pious foundation.[72] He is given discretionary power in the matter of accepting or rejecting these foundations, and no persona moralis[73] can accept a foundation without his written consent. He has the further right and duty to designate the place where the money or goods constituting the endowment shall be deposited and to see that the funds are wisely invested, after consultation with the diocesan board of administration and others who are interested.[74]

In order to facilitate the business administration of his diocese, the Ordinary is instructed, after consulting the chapter (or consultors) to appoint a board of administrators consisting of himself as president and two or three competent men who have some knowledge of civil law; but this need not be done in places where particular law or custom provides an equally effective mode of administration.[75]

---

[68] Canons 1530, 1532, § 2 and 3.
[69] Canon 1532, § 4.
[70] Canon 1532, § 2.
[71] Canon 105.
[72] Canon 1545.
[73] Except exempt religious—Canon 1550.
[74] Canon 1547.
[75] Canon 1520.

In addition to the diocesan board of administrators, the Ordinary should appoint a board of administrators for each individual place, unless such administrators already exist by law or charter; the members of this board should hold office for only three years unless local circumstances make a longer or shorter term advisable.[76]

It is needless to state that in the matter of appointing pastors, creating new parishes, etc., the bishop is supreme. These are spiritual matters, and the bishop rules his diocese iure divino. There is, however, a special case where temporalities are involved. Where a new parish is created by dividing an old one, the question may arise as to how much property, if any, the old church should contribute to the new one. This is a matter for the Ordinary alone to determine unless, in exceptional cases, there is some special condition attached to the property. He should, however, be guided by a sense of justice and by the equities of a given situation.[77]

(*c*) *The Pastor.*—The pastor, by virtue of his office as beneficiary, is the administrator of all property belonging to the benefice.[78] He is, however, bound to observe the rules of administration laid down in the Code[79] and is bound to restitution for losses sustained by the church through any fault or neglect on his part.[80] Though empowered to administer the property in his own name,[81] he is held strictly accountable to the bishop, and he may be removed from office for maladministration.[82]

(*d*) *The Laity.*—The laity have no right under the general law to interfere in the administration of ecclesiastical property. It is possible, however, to have lay administrators in individual cases. There is nothing to prevent the Ordinary from appointing laymen to act on the diocesan board of administrators,[83] and they may also be members of the special boards mentioned in Canon 1521.

---

76 Canon 1521.

77 Canon 1427, § 3, and Canon 1500.

78 Canon 1476, § 1, and Canon 1410.

79 Cfr. e. g. Canon 1523, etc.

80 Canon 1476, § 2.

81 Fanfani, *De Iure Parochorum,* 159.

82 Canon 1476, 2147, . . .

83 Canon 1520, Augustine, *Commentary,* VI, 581.

Canon 1521.

§ 1. Praeter hoc diocesanum consilium administrationis. Ordinarius loci in administrationem bonorum quae ad aliquam ecclesiam vel locum pium pertinent et ex iure vel tabulis fundationis suum non habent administratorem, assumat viros providos, idoneos et boni testimonii, quibus, elapso triennio, alios sufficiat, nisi locorum circumstantiae aliud suadeant.

§ 2. Quod si laicis partes quaedam in administratione bonorum ecclesiasticorum vel ex legitimo fundationis seu erectionis titulo vel ex Ordinarii loci voluntate competant, nihilominus universa administratio nomine Ecclesiae flat, ac salvo iure Ordinarii visitandi, exigendi rationes et praescribendi modum administrationis.

The point to be stressed in interpreting the first paragraph of this canon is that this paragraph refers to the appointment of administrators in those exceptional cases where the law itself or the provisions of a foundation do not stipulate who shall be the administrator. The word ecclesia in this part of the Code is a general term that may include any persona moralis;[84] it does not necessarily mean a church. In a properly erected parish, the law itself[85] stipulates that the pastor shall administer all property destined for the upkeep of the church and the carrying on of divine services, as well as all offerings made for the use of the parish. Canon 1521, 1, would therefore seem to have a more important bearing on hospitals, cemeteries, etc., than on strictly parochial enterprises. In these exceptional cases it is manifest from the wording of the canon that the Ordinary may appoint either clerics or laymen, provided they have the proper qualifications.

Where laymen have a share in the administration of parochial property, whether by stipulation of the founder, by the will of the Ordinary, or by custom,[86] they act merely as agents of the church, and are amenable to the Ordinary, who has the right of visitation, of demanding

[84] Canon 1498.

[85] Canon 1182—2. It might be noted, however, that this Canon makes exception in favor of special administrators already existing, as also of particular laws and legitimate customs.

[86] Cfr. Canon 1182.

a regular accounting and of prescribing the mode of administration. It is hardly necessary to mention that lay administrators have no control over spiritual matters.[87]

It is needless to enter further into the question of dominion over parochial property. The treatment already given, though superficial from the canonical standpoint, is ample for the purpose of this thesis. It shows that various forms of control usually included under the name of dominion are, in canon law, not focused in a single individual, but exercised by various persons under varying conditions. If, under civil law, an owner is generally presumed to have full control over his property, it is at once apparent that the civil tenure of parochial property will present many difficulties, in places where the personality of the Church, with its own legal system, is not given complete recognition by the civil power. To inquire into the various methods of circumventing some of these difficulties will be the next step in this thesis.

[87] Canon 1521, §2, 154, 166, etc.

CHAPTER VII.

THE BISHOP AS ABSOLUTE OWNER.

"As a last resource, the bishop may hold the temporal goods of the diocese and administer them in his individual name, under that absolue title of law which in English is called a fee simple; in which case let the bishop be always mindful, that, although the full ownership of ecclesiastical property is given him by the civil law, nevertheless according to the admonitions of the sacred canons he is not the owner of it but only the administrator."[1]

Before attempting to examine this part of the decree, it will not be out of place to describe what is meant in English law by the term fee simple. By a strange anomaly, difficult to understand, ecclesiastical writers sometimes use this term as if it were the key word of the part of the decree under consideration. Thus Baart[2] constantly speaks of the fee simple tenure of bishops, and Augustine[3] in pointing out the different forms of holding church property says: "They are: (a) by corporation sole . . . (b) by corporation aggregate . . . (c) in fee simple which conveys absolute and direct ownership of the property, and was looked upon in former days as vested in the bishop for all diocesan property."

As a matter of fact, fee simple is not a kind of tenure but a degree of an estate.[4] Moreover, a corporation, aggregate or sole, and a trustee, as well as an individual holding for himself, can and must have the fee simple in landed property if his estate is to be unlimited. Finally the term fee simple applies only to lands, tenements and hereditaments, and has nothing to do with movable goods. All this

[1] Concl. Plenarium Balt. III, Tit. IX, cap. ii, n. 267.

[2] *The Tenure of Catholic Church Property*, 66, . . .

[3] *Commentary*, VI, 557, 558.

[4] Tenure has to do with the manner of holding property, while an estate signifies "such an interest as the tenant hath herein." Blackstone, *Commentaries*, II, 103.

will appear from an examination of the meaning of the term.

Blackstone divides estates in land, with regard to the quantity of interest, into "such as are freehold and such as are less than freehold."[5] A freehold estate, stripped of technicalities, is an estate that endures at least for the life of an individual.[6] Estates of freehold "are either estates of inheritance, or estates not of inheritance. The former are again divided into inheritance absolute or fee simple; and inheritance limited, one species of which we usually call fee tail."

"Tenant in fee simple," he continues, "is he that hath land, tenements, or hereditaments to hold to him and his heirs forever; generally absolutely, and simply; without mentioning what heirs, but referring that to his own pleasure, or to the disposition of the law."[7] . . . "The word 'heirs' is necessary in the grant or donation, in order to make a fee or inheritance. For if land be given to a man forever, or to him and his assigns forever, this vests in him but an estate for life. This very great nicety about the insertion of the word 'heirs' in all feoffments and grants, in order to vest a fee, is plainly a relic of the feudal strictness, by which, we may remember, it was required that the form of the donation should be punctually pursued; or that, as Crag expresses it in the words of Baldus, 'donationes sint stricti iuris, ne quis plus donasse praesumatur quam in donatione expresserit.' And, therefore, as the personal abilities of the donee were supposed to be the only inducements to the gift, the donee's estate in the land extended only to his own person, and subsisted no longer than his life; unless the donor, by an expressed provision in the grant, gave it a longer continuance, and extended it also to his heirs."[8] In contradistinction to fee simple there are "limited fees, or such estates of inheritance as are clogged and confined with conditions, or qualifications of any sort."[9]

To complete the notion of an estate in fee simple it is

---

[5] l. c.

[6] Blackstone, *Commentaries,* II, 120.—Clark, *Outlines,* 263.

[7] Blackstone, *Commentaries,* II, 104.

[8] Ibid. 107.

[9] Ibid. 108.

necessary to refer to the famous Rule in Shelley's Case which held "that when the ancestor, by any gift or conveyance, taketh an estate of freehold, and the same gift or estate is limited, either immediately or mediately, to his heirs, in fee or in tail, the heirs are words of limitation of the estate, and not words of purchase."[10] This means that, although on the face of the deed it would appear that the heirs had an interest in the estate, the heirs are not to be considered purchasers, and the ancestor can alienate the estate if he chooses to do so; the word "heirs" is presumed to be used as a "word of limitation," that is, a word denoting the quantity of the estate. Nevertheless, the estate remains an estate of inheritance, and if not alienated during life, or by testamentary disposition, will descend, at the death of the ancestor, to his heirs, general or special, as the case may be.

To sum up the above in a practical way: The law of real property is encrusted with feudal ideas which require a strictly technical interpretation of deeds to land. In consequence of this, if "A" conveys lands merely to "B" or "to 'B' forever" or "to 'B' and his assigns forever," "B" takes only a life estate, with the remainder in "A" and his heirs. In order for "A" to convey absolute and unlimited title, the deed must be "to 'B' and his heirs forever" and "B" then has an estate in fee simple. It may not be amiss to point out that where land is conveyed to a corporation sole the fee may be passed by substituting the word "successors" for the word "heirs," for as Blackstone says "as heirs take from an ancestor, so doth the successor from the predecessor."[11] Similarly, "in a grant of land to a corporation aggregate the word 'successors' is not necessary, though usually inserted; for, albeit such simple grant be strictly only an estate for life, yet, as that corporation never dies, such estate for life is perpetual, or equivalent to fee simple, and therefore the law allows it to be one."[12]

To return to the decree. If the term "fee simple" is to be interpreted technically, this part of the decree applies

[10] Kent, *Commentaries,* IV, 215.—Blackstone, *Commentaries,* II, 172.
[11] Blackstone, *Commentaries,* II, 108.
[12] Ibid.

only to real property, while the rest of the decree seems to provide for both real and personal property. A corporation, whether aggregate or sole, can own both realty and movable goods, and the *res* of a trust can be either real, or personal. But what of movable goods under the last part of the decree? Churches, schools, parochial residences, etc., would present no difficulty. Being permanently attached to the soil, they would be considered part of the realty, and held in the name of the bishop. Altars, baptismal fonts, vestment cases and other fixtures would, in all probability, follow the same rule. But precious vessels, vestments, books, bonds, money in bank, and everything of a movable nature, would, in time of litigation, be left to the disposition of the civil courts. This was evidently not the mind of the council. Why, then, did it use the term fee simple?

It is suggested that the council, in using this term, might have been intent upon preventing loose methods of securing real estate. A layman in the law might naturally think that a deed "to the bishop of 'B' and his successors in office" would pass title to the bishop's successors at his death. As a matter of fact, the property would vest in the donor or his heirs, since the deed conveyed only an estate for life. But if the same layman in the law knew that the bishop had to hold the property in fee simple, he would probably consult a lawyer and have the deed drawn up in proper form.

Whatever might have been the reason of the council for using the term "fee simple," it is respectfully submitted that the term was not intended as the key word to this part of the decree, and it is better to speak of "the bishop as absolute owner" than of "fee simple tenure by the bishop." The real tenor of this part of the decree is that the bishop holds "in his individual name" in such a way that "the full ownership of ecclesiastical property is given him by the civil law." It must be borne in mind, however, (1) that the council intended the arrangement only as a last resort, and (2) that the arrangement is purely a civil one, and according to canon law the bishop is only the administrator of the property.

The chief advantage of making the bishop the absolute

owner of church property under the civil law, is that this prevents undue interference in church affairs on the part of the laity. This, in fact, was the reason why the arrangement was first adopted.

At the beginning of the nineteenth century most of the property of the Church in the United States was held or administered by the lay trustees.[13] The reason is not difficult to understand. On the one hand, small communities of Catholics being without the services of resident priests would build their own churches and then endeavor to secure priests to visit their places as missionaries; these people naturally had to take care of their church property in the absence of the missionaries.[14] On the other hand, many of the Catholics in the United States were from countries in continental Europe where church property was administered by the Fabriques, and these were insistent on having their old world customs introduced in America; they did not understand that in their native land the attitude of the civil law toward the peculiar constitution of the Church was well settled, while in America it had yet to be determined.[15] Again the Catholic people who were but a small minority were surrounded by Protestant sects organized on a basis of lay control with a clergy that was removable at the will of the people. The law naturally growing out of the customs of the majority, permitted congregations to hold property, but insisted that the trustees be elected by the people.[16] Archbishop Carroll, wishing where possible to harmonize the administration of church affairs with the American principle of democracy, instituted the system of lay trustees in Catholic congregations, and other bishops followed his example.[17]

For nearly half a century after the establishment of lay trusteeship, the Church in the United States was harassed by internal dissensions, which greatly impeded the progress of the faith, and sometimes threatened to sever

[13] Baart, o. c., 25.

[14] MacCaffrey: *History of the Catholic Church in the Nineteenth Century*, II, 279.

[15] Ibid.

[16] Ibid.

[17] Ibid.—Baart, o. c., 21.

entire communities from the body of the faithful. Trustees, not content with merely sharing in the administration of temporal affairs, attempted to dictate to priests and bishops in matters spiritual. They refused to accept the services of lawfully appointed priests and insisted on retaining priests of their own choice, sometimes, unfortunately, encouraged by the latter. In many instances their quarrels were carried to the civil courts and sometimes even to Rome.

As early as 1822, the Holy See undertook to condemn the abuses of the trustee system, pointing out that the bishops, by divine appointment, preside over their respective churches, and cannot be excluded from the care, superintendence and administration of church property. The Holy See did not condemn the system itself, nor did it direct the bishops to assume entire control. It merely pointed out the faults of the system and laid down certain regulations that were to be followed in future in order to protect the interest of the Church.[18]

In spite of the efforts of the Holy See to secure peace, the trouble continued, and it became evident to the bishops that more drastic methods were necessary. In 1829 the First Provincial Council of Baltimore therefore enacted the following decree:

"Since lay trustees have too often abused the power given them by the civil law to the great detriment of religion and not without scandal to the faithful, we very greatly desire that in the future no church shall be built or consecrated, unless it shall have been assigned by written instrument to the bishop in whose diocese it is to be built, wherever this can be done. . . ."[19]

This decree was immediately carried out, and was virtually incorporated in most of the diocesan statutes of that period.

The result of this method of tenure was beneficial on the whole, and the Church, no longer hampered by the trustee system, made great progress under the leadership

---

[18] Pius VII, litt. ap. *Non sine magno*, 24 aug. 1822, *Fontes*, n. 480.

[19] Translation of Baart, p. 53.

of a zealous episcopal body.[20] Nevertheless, the bishops themselves soon began to doubt the advisability of the system. Dangers were recognized, particularly in regard to the transfer of property at the time of the bishop's death.[21] In 1837 the Third Provincial Council[22] insisted on the necessity of properly securing movable and immovable property, and the Fourth Provincial Council, 1840, added[23] "that if this security can be obtained in no other way, then the property is to be handed down by means of last wills and testaments, drawn up according to the provisions of the civil law." The Propaganda[24] the same year issued a decree directing each bishop to make a will in favor of a fellow bishop, instructing the latter in a separate document, afterwards to be burned, that the property should be transferred to the successor of the testator. The Fathers of the Fifth Provincial Council, 1843, declared this decree of the Propaganda to be difficult of execution and asked[25] that it be modified to the effect that each bishop, within three months after his consecration, make a will and deposit a duplicate of it in the office of the archbishop. In 1855 the New York Legislature enacted a statute (repealed in 1863) providing that no title to real property should be conveyable or descendible by an ecclesiastic to his successor in office, and there are traces of similar legislation in other states.[26] In 1868 the European relatives of Bishop Baraga contested his will and had to be bought off.[27] In 1879 Archbishop Purcell, of Cincinnati, was forced to make an assignment for the benefit of his creditors who tried to levy on the property of the church,[28] and the case was still in the courts when the Third Plenary Council met in 1884. This council therefore enacted that the method of making the bishop the absolute owner of Church property was to

[20] Baart, o. c., 56.
[21] Baart, o. c., 57.
[22] N. 43.
[23] N. 56.
[24] 15 Dec. 1840, Collect. S. Cong. de Prop. Fide, n. 916.
[25] N. 59.
[26] Desmond, *The Church and the Law,* 70, 71.
[27] Baart, p. 68.
[28] Mannix v. Purcell, 46 O. S., 102.

be used only as a last resort.[29] Finally, the Sacred Congregation of the Council, by decree of July 29, 1911, forbade the method entirely.[30]

Before one can form an adequate judgment as to the advisability of making the bishop absolute owner of Church property in a particular state, he must know how the law of the state in question regards this system of tenure. There are two classes of decisions on this point, one adhering strictly to the wording of the deed, the other declaring a trust to exist, in spite of the fact that no trust is expressed in the instrument of conveyance. Examples of each are submitted.

(1) *Cases where no trust was deemed to exist.*—"Certain members of the local society being dissatisfied with the management of the property, brought an action against the bishop for the purpose of obtaining some part in the control of the property, alleging that the property was acquired by contributions from the people under circumstances which created a trust. The legal title had been conveyed to the bishop without any provision creating a trust, and under the law of the Church the property was held for the use of the congregation who attended public worship therein. The plaintiffs were not entitled to the relief sought."[31]

"In Heiss v. Vosburg, 59 Wis., 532, it appeared that in 1866 the trustees of Sinsinawa Mound College conveyed certain real estate, on which there was a church building, to the bishop of Milwaukee for the nominal consideration of one dollar. It also appeared that the bishop devised this property to his official successor, who brought this action, claiming that the defendants had unlawfully entered on the premises, torn down and removed the building thereon and were digging up and removing the soil for the purpose of laying the foundations for a new building which they threatened to erect against his wish and protests. The defendants who were members of the Roman Catholic Church at Sinsinawa Mound, known at St. Dominic's

[29] Concl .Plen. Balt. III, Tit. IX, cap. ii, n. 167.

[30] Ecc. Rev., Nov., 1911, 591–596; Micheletti, *Ius Pianum*, 334, 335.

[31] Hennessey v. Walsh, 55 N. H., 515.—Lincoln, o. c., 664.

Church, claimed that the church building was originally erected by funds and materials furnished by the congregation, and that it had been practically under the control of trustees chosen by the congregation since 1866; also that the deed to the bishop was in trust for the congregation. The courts held that the original deed to the bishop was absolute and conveyed a fee simple title, leaving nothing in the congregation or the trustees thereof, and that they had no interest in the property. Neither the congregation nor the trustees could lawfully tear down the church building, even for the purpose of erecting a new one, against the protest of the bishop who held the legal title, and who had control of the property under the law of the Church."[82]

(2) *Cases where trusts were deemed to exist.*—"Where property is purchased by a congregation for a special purpose, although the deed is made to the bishop, the congregation is entitled to control the property, and the bishop holds the property in trust for the congregation.—Fink v. Umscheid, 40 Kan., 271."[83]

"From the statements contained in the opinion of the Supreme Court of Ohio (Mannix vs. Purcell, 46 Ohio St., 102), it appears that Father Edward Purcell, brother of Archbishop Purcell, of Cincinnati, had for many years (from 1837–1879) been receiving deposits from individual Catholics, who preferred to trust him as their banker rather than deposit their funds in the banks. The canon laws of the Church forbade this to be done by an ecclesiastic. Father Purcell, however, acted, with the consent of his brother, in the matter, and the latter, in his individual capacity, assumed the entire indebtedness. Both made assignments to Mannix early in 1879, and the claims, proved up to the assignee, amounted to about $2,500,000.00. It was sought to charge two hundred pieces of church property in the Cincinnati archdiocese with the unpaid portion of this indebtedness. The title to this property was in John B. Purcell, the archbishop, in fee simple; but the supreme court admitted parol testimony and the canons and decrees of the Catholic Church regulating the manner

82 Lincoln, o. c., 664, 665.
83 Lincoln, o. c., 664.

of acquiring and holding church property, as competent evidence to show that Archbishop Purcell held this property in trust for religious and charitable purposes. It was held that the property as held in trust by the Archbishop did not pass to his assignee in insolvency for the payment of his individual debts, such as the indebtedness in question was (with some exceptions) held to be."[34]

The above cases are sufficient to indicate that various courts are apt to take diverse views of the bishop's tenure under a deed that purports to make him the absolute owner. While the Statute of Frauds[35] and the general rules of evidence[36] render it difficult to change the face of a deed there is always the possibility that the doctrine of resulting trusts or constructive trusts[37] may be applied by courts of equity. Where the courts of a certain state have never been called upon to decide the question, the view they might take is a matter of conjecture, and it is not possible to decide the point, as an attempt has been made to do, on the fact that "in most states no parole evidence can be admitted to contest the reading of deeds."[38]

In states where the courts have extended the doctrine of trusts to deeds that on their face confer absolute ownership upon the bishop, it is ventured that the prohibition of the Congregation of the Council does not apply; otherwise the Congregation would have forbidden the bishops to hold church property in trust; for it is of little consequence whether a trust is written into a deed by the grantor or read into it by the courts. The remainder of the chapter will therefore be devoted to the case where no trust of any nature is deemed to exist, by the courts.

The absolute title in the name of the bishop, though now forbidden by the law of the Church, does not appear to be so void of merit as some of its opponents maintain. Its advantages, as well as its defects, can be learned from a critical examination of some of the arguments urged against it. These arguments are taken from Baart, who

[34] Reported by Humphrey J. Desmond, o. c., 103.
[35] Kent, *Commentaries*, IV, 450, 452.
[36] Kent, *Commentaries*, II, 556.
[37] Kent, *Commentaries*, IV, 450.
[38] Baart, o. c., 66.

maintained that this form of tenure is "unnecessary, unsafe, unwise, expensive, and detrimental to the best interests of the Church in the United States."[39]

(1) "The individual tenure in bishops is an actual alienation of all church property so held, and in realty as foreign to the spirit of the Church as lay trusteeism."

Answer:—Granted that this is an alienation, it follows that every other system of tenure is an alienation. A persona moralis holds the property under church law, and even if the state incorporates a parish, this corporation is a creature of the law of the state, and is not identical with the ecclesiastical persona moralis. This system is opposed to the spirit of the Church if Church law regards the bishop as the owner of the property; but Baart himself admits that "Bishops do not own parish property before the canon law,"[40] and it should not be assumed that any bishop has the intent to defraud the Church. The Church, by permitting the bishop to be the depository of the civil title, is not thereby taking the property away from the persona moralis that legitimately acquired it.[41] The Church is a divine institution, and the bishop is bound by her laws, even though the state refuses to recognize this obligation.

(2) "The civil title to church property should correspond as nearly as possible with the canonical title."

Answer:—Since the civil and canonical personality can never be identical under our laws, the correspondence should be sought in the method of administering the property. Where the bishop is the absolute owner under the civil law, he is free under the civil law to put all the Church canons into effect. He is not amenable to courts of equity as he would be if he were a trustee; and he is not bound by the civil law to accept as final the proceedings of a board of administration, as he would be if this board were the trustees of a corporation. It is therefore ventured that this method of tenure, presuming that the bishop is con-

---

[39] Baart, o. c., 60, . . .

[40] Baart, o. c., 60.

[41] For an interesting discussion of a condition similar to this, see article "De Licentia Requisita Ad Hoc Ut Religiosus Votorum Sollemnium Possit Actus Proprietatis In Foro Civili Nomine Proprio Exercere," in the Commentarium Pro Religiosis, IV, 266–272; V, 10–20; 94–98; 270–272; 378–389.

scientious, corresponds as nearly as possible to the prescriptions of canon law.

(3) "It is not only good policy, but it is the spirit of the Church to adapt herself to the circumstances of the country wherein she exists, provided no sin or forfeiture of principle is the consequence. Hence, in the tenure of church property she should at least not antagonize the general sentiment and practice of the country, unless this sentiment and practice are entirely wrong."

Answer:—There need be no antagonism to the general sentiment and practice of the country if the bishop appoints a consilium fabricae,[42] or board of administrators. Should the bishop overstep his rights, this board, it is true, would have no redress in the secular courts, but it is not the intention of the Church that they should.[43] On the other hand, they would have redress at canon law.[44]

(4) "One-man power is diametrically opposed to the spirit and institutions of this country. . . . All canon law shows that one-man power is opposed also to the spirit of the Church."

Answer:—This argument seems to take for granted that the bishop is going to use the so-called one-man power as a sword instead of a shield—that because the Church cannot use the secular arm to enforce her rights, the bishop is going to disregard the canons of the Church, and become arbitrary in the administration of her property. An arrangement whereby one-man power is conferred on the bishop by the civil law, even if permitted by the Church, would not confer one-man power under canon law. On the other hand, one-man power is an excellent thing if used merely as a check upon the usurpation of power by trustees.

The arguments given above amount to nothing more than this: if the Church were to permit the bishop to have the absolute title to property in those places where the courts would not declare the bishop a trustee, the Church would be without redress in case the bishop were to convert the property to his own use.

---

[42] Canon 1183.

[43] Canon 120, 123, 2341.

[44] Canon 1653, § 4.

Inasmuch as the Church, in placing a bishop over a diocese, entrusts him with interests immeasurably more important than property rights, it is questionable whether the above arguments have much weight. But there are other objections against this system, that are more worthy of consideration.

(1) "In the first place, in spite of all wish to the contrary, the owner of all Church property, the bishop, is liable for all the debts on any piece of parish property. On the other hand, if he becomes bankrupt, each and every piece of church property is liable for all his debts. . . . The fee simple system makes it possible for the bishop to mortgage property of one parish for the benefit of schools, seminaries or churches of other parishes. It makes it possible for the bishop to divert property from the object for which it was given to another very different one." etc.[45]

In places where the courts would not declare the bishop a trustee, this objection has some weight, even if a little bit far-fetched. It is not impossible to conceive of a bishop, in his zeal for the welfare of souls in his diocese, undertaking financial obligations which he is later unable to meet.[46] In this case the property of the entire diocese might suffer.

(2) "During a vacancy caused by the death of a bishop, who owns the property? Every power of attorney given by the deceased bishop expires, and who can collect rents or sue to put out tenants of parish property? Who can collect insurance in case of fire, and in whose name are policies to be written? Who can give proper security for necessary loans or for the renewal of previous authorized loans? Will the probate court appoint or confirm an executor? What bonds shall he give, and who will furnish them? . . ."[47]

It is obvious that the above questions might require as many answers as there are states in the union, multiplied by the number of conditions that might be put in a will. Nevertheless, they are practical and pertinent questions,

[45] Baart, o. c., 69.

[46] It must be remembered, however, that canon law limits the bishop's power to mortgage property.—Canons 1538, 1532, etc.

[47] Baart, o. c., 69.

and apt to cause serious complications. If the testator can direct that the executor act without bond, and if the executor can mortgage property with the consent of the probate court, perhaps most of these difficulties will vanish. But all this will depend on local laws and on the skill with which the bishop's will is drawn; and there would probably be untold difficulties, no matter how favorable the local laws might be.

(3) "In the case the bishop dies leaving a will which disposes of church property as canon law and conscience require. What assurance have we that such a testament will stand? It may be contested on various grounds, and experience teaches that few wills which are contested remain unbroken. We will suppose that a will has been legally and carefully drawn, which is not always the case; what is to prevent a bishop from making a later will, either through favoritism, disgust, disappointment or revenge, all of which are characteristics of a failing mind? And if, unfortunately, a bishop should make such a will, what can be done about it?"[48]

This objection is undoubtedly the weightiest one that can be urged against placing absolute title in the name of a bishop. The property, according to law, belongs not to the church but to the bishop. If the bishop dies intestate, or if his will be broken, the property will pass to his heirs under the statutes of descent and distribution. If through feeble mindedness he makes a second will alienating the property of the Church, the second will may be broken but the property will still go to the heirs. It will be extremely difficult, if at all possible, to break the second will and to maintain the first.

To sum up: In the early days of the Republic the Church suffered a great deal from the abuses of lay trustees of church property. In order to remedy this condition, the bishops insisted on having the absolute title to church property in themselves. While the Church profited by this system of tenure, it had serious disadvantages. The Third Plenary Council of Baltimore therefore decreed that it be used only as a last resort, and the Sacred Congregation of

[48] Ibid., 66, 67.

the Council[49] finally forbade it entirely; but this prohibition probably does not extend to places where it is certain that the courts consider the bishop a trustee. Absolute title in the bishop makes it possible for the bishop himself to have all the laws of the Church with regard to property carried out in their fullest details as long as the bishop lives; but it causes difficulties when the bishop dies, and is apt to result in the total loss of all property to the Church.

[49] Eccl. Rev., Nov., 1911, 591–596; Micheletti, *Ius Pianum,* 334, 335.

CHAPTER VIII.

The Bishop as Trustee.

"The property of the diocese . . . may be committed to the bishop in trust that he may hold it in the name of the diocese and administer it according to the wish of the Church."[1]

A trust may be defined as a right of property held by one person, called the trustee, for the benefit of another called the beneficiary, or the *cestui qui trust.*[2] In English jurisprudence, the trust is a development of what was formerly known as a "use."

A use originally was nothing more than a confidence placed in a friend to whom property had been given for the benefit of a third party. The interest of the third party, or the *cestui qui use,* was dependent on the honesty of the trustee, or feoffee to use, who was the legal owner; and the *cestui* had no remedy at common law if the feoffee violated the confidence placed in him. With the establishment of the courts of chancery, however, the moral obligation of the feoffee was recognized and would be enforced in equity.[3]

Upon the passage of the various statutes of Mortmain, the effect of which was to make grants of lands to corporations absolutely void, it became the custom for those wishing to convey property to the Church, to make a conveyance to a physical person for the use of the Church. This was not deemed to be a conveyance to the Church itself; the grant was, therefore, valid; the grantee, not being a corporation, could take the title, but the court of chancery,

---

[1] Concl. Plenarium Balt. III, Tit. IX, cap. ii, n. 267.

[2] Cochran: *The Students' Law Lexicon,* v. *trust.*

[3] Blackstone: o. c., II, 327 seqq.—Kent: o. c., IV, 290 seqq.—Clark: *Outlines,* 270 to 272.

the chancellor himself being an ecclesiastic,[4] would compel the feoffee to hold the estate to the use of the Church.[5]

In order to prevent the Church from obtaining the use of property, the "Statute for Transferring Uses into Possession" was passed in the reign of Henry VIII (1535). This statute provided that whoever possessed the use of property, should also be vested with the legal title. Property then destined for the use of the Church, would have to be vested in the Church, and since the Church, under the Statutes of Mortmain, was incapable of holding the legal title, the grant for the use of the Church was void.[6]

It then became the custom to convey property to one physical person, for the use of a second physical person, for the use of the Church. Common law courts adopted the principle that a use could not be limited upon a use; they would not recognize the title as passing, by the Statute of Uses, any further than the second physical person, deeming the limitation of the use to be void. The chancellor, however, would compel the second physical person to hold in trust for the Church. The trust was, therefore, a use limited upon a use, but later on the intermediate use was no longer deemed necessary in order to convey property in trust.[7]

Wherever a trust exists, there are two distinct titles to the property. The legal title, and the only one recognized at law, is vested in the trustee; the law places no restrictions on his disposition of the property. The equitable title, however, is vested in the *cestui qui trust,* or those for whose use the property is destined; and the courts of equity will always compel the trustee to carry out the conditions of the trust. Thus, in practice, the arrangement is almost the same as though the *cestui qui trust* were the owner of the property, and the trustee the administrator.

Where the bishop of a diocese holds the parochial property in trust, the arrangement may be said to have most

---

[4] It was not until the reign of Edward III (A. D. 1340) that the first lay chancellor was appointed.—Strong: *Relations of Civil Law to Church Polity,* 83.

[5] See authorities in note 3.

[6] Ibid.

[7] Ibid.

of the advantages of the system of absolute ownership by the bishop, without any of its dangers. The bishop in this case has the legal title to the property, and as its legal owner he can administer the property in such a manner that all the canons of the Church are carried out in their most minute details. He can place the property in the hands of a board of administrators, while at the same time being free to remove an administrator if he sees fit. He can always superintend the administration of the property, as canon law directs him to do[8] and can check all unreasonable acts of the administrators, since they are only his agents under the civil law. On the other hand, the property of the Church is not endangered. Should the bishop suffer financial reverses, and become insolvent, the property of the Church could not be levied upon by his creditors.[9] Should he die without making a will,[10] the property would not descend to his heirs, since the *cestui qui trust* is the equitable owner.

Considering the arrangement from another point of view, it approximates the system of tenure under canon law. In canon law, the property, e. g., of St. Mary's Church belongs to a *persona moralis non-collegialis*. The rector of St. Mary's Church is the administrator through whom this moral person must act, while the bishop has the duty of supervising this administration.[11] The property itself, though belonging to a *persona moralis non-collegialis* and administered by the rector under the supervision of the bishop, is destined primarily for the spiritual good of the people of St. Mary's parish. In American civil law, though the owner of property held in trust by the bishop is not a *persona moralis non-collegialis,* the same effect is secured by separating the legal and equitable title. The bishop administers the property, but it is destined for the spiritual good of the people. Now the bishop can legally (according to civil law) make the rector of the church his agent in the administration of the property, but the acts of this rector as agent will always be under the bishop's super-

---

8 Canon 1520.

9 Cfr., e. g. Mannix v. Purcell, 46 Ohio St., 102.

10 Strong, o. c., 105.

11 Supra, Chapter VI.

vision.[12] In this case, both in canon and civil law, the rector administers the property, the bishop supervises the administration, and the property itself is used for the spiritual good of the parish. The only difference under the two systems of law is that under canon law the property is held by a *persona moralis*, while under civil law the legal title is in the bishop and the equitable title in the people; but this difference is merely theoretical, and is due to the fact that in English law the trust fund was never personified.

That much advantage accrues to the Church where her property is held in trust cannot be questioned. As has already been pointed out,[13] it practically gives the Church rights under civil law which she would otherwise not possess, having no civil personality. It forever prevents the conversion of church property to the use of a schismatic sect, even where an entire congregation becomes schismatic.[14] It would in fact be the ideal method of tenure were it not for the absolute control that the civil courts assume over all trusts.

To give an adequate idea of the extent to which this control is exercised would be quite impossible. The following quotation from Zollmann[15] is submitted as covering the most important points:

"While some courts have held that the bishop, if a trustee, is an active trustee, entitled to enjoin members of the congregation with whose funds the property has been bought from erecting a building (Foley v. Kleibusch, 123 Mich. 416; 82 N. W., 223) or to recover damages from such members for tearing down a building on it (Heiss v. Vosburg, 59 Wis., 532; 18 N. W., 463), while such property in the absence of a 'legally enforcible trust' for a religious association has been held not to be exempt from taxation (Katzer v. Milwaukee, 104 Wis., 16; 79 N. W., 745, 80 N. W., 41), and while courts have refused to declare a trust [Here he is referring to cases where no trust is expressed in the deed] or give directions to the bishop in cases where

[12] Zollmann, o. c., 353.
[13] Supra, Chapter V.
[14] Supra, Chapter V.
[15] o. c., 355, 356.

no misconduct of any kind on the part of the bishop was alleged and plaintiffs constituted a very small minority of the congregation (Hennesey v. Walsh, 55 N. H., 515; Determan v. Luehrsimann, 74 Iowa, 275; 37 N. W., 330); the rule established by the best considered cases is that the bishop is a mere dry, passive, silent trustee without any interest or power (Carrick v. Canevin, 90 Atl., 147 (Pa.); O'Hear v. De Goesbriand, 33 Vt., 593; 80 Am. Dec., 653; Kranczunas v. Hogan, 221 Pa., 13; 70 Atl., 740; Mazaika v. Kranczunas, 233 Pa., 138; 81 Atl., 938. See also Kenrick v. Cole, 61 Mo., 572.), while each separate congregation, as distinct from the other congregations in the same diocese (Mannix v. Purcell, 46 Ohio St., 102; 19 N. E., 572; 2 L. R. A., 753; 15 Am. St. Rep., 562; Searle v. Bishop of Springfield, 203 Mass., 493; 89 N. E., 809), is the real, actual, beneficial owner of the property (Carrick Borough v. Canevin, 90 Atl., 147; O'Hear v. De Goesbriand, 332, 593; 80 Am. Dec., 653. See also Kenrick v. Cole, 61 Mo., 572; Kranczunas v. Hoban, 221 Pa., 213, 221; 70 Atl. 740), which ownership is of such value that it may form the consideration for a contract (Arts v. Guthrie, 75 Iowa, 674; 37 N. W., 395), and gives the congregation the right to sell unqualified by any right in the trustee. (Neeley v. Hoskins, 84 Me., 386; 24 Atl., 882. See also Armour v. Spalding, 14 Colo., 302; 23 Pac. 789) . . . It further follows that on the death of the bishop the court may appoint a trustee in his stead. (In re St. George v. Lithuanian Roman Catholic Church, 90 Atl., 918.)"

Thus the courts have so minimized the importance of the bishop's office as trustee, as to make the bishop a mere depository of the legal title, subject entirely to the will of the *cestui qui trust*. The extent to which this doctrine may at times be stretched by the courts is well exemplified by a Pennsylvania case which was carried to the Supreme Court of that state no less than five times. The case is ably reviewed by Zollmann[16] but will be summarized here because of the light it throws on the question under discussion.

In 1906 the congregation of St. Joseph's Lithuanian

[16] o. c., 357 to 361.

Church, of Scranton, Pennsylvania, passed a resolution authorizing certain of its members to bring action against the bishop to force him to convey to them the property which he held in his own name as "trustee for the St. Joseph Lithuanian Catholic Congregation." There was at the time a statute in Pennsylvania to the effect that property taken by anyone for the use of the Church "shall not be otherwise taken and held, or inure, than subject to the control and disposition of the lay members of such church."

The members authorized by the congregation brought the action which ultimately came before the Supreme Court in 1908. This court decided that "the defendant [Bishop Hoban] is trustee of the legal title to the property for the exclusive use of said congregation, without any interest therein or any right or power to control its disposition; the congregation has the right to substitute other trustees in his stead, and, having done so by a majority vote at a regularly called meeting for that purpose, it is entitled to the process of the court to compel a conveyance to the trustees of its own selection." It was also held that the canons of the Church were in conflict with the statute referred to in the last paragraph. Whether the absence of such a statute would have varied the decision is a matter of conjecture.

The bishop made the conveyance as ordered by the court, but ex-communicated the trustees and placed the church under an interdict. The congregation therefore held another meeting, sixteen hundred voters being present, and passed a resolution to choose and designate the bishop as "trustee for said St. Joseph's Lithuanian Catholic Congregation of the city of Scranton, Pennsylvania, to hold as such trustee all the property of said congregation and the title thereto in accordance with the laws, rules and usages of the Catholic Church."

A reconveyance was then ordered by the chancellor, but only after an election lasting ten days had been held in open court, the trustees having contested the validity of the resolution passed at the meeting of the congregation. The case was immediately appealed to the Supreme Court.

The Supreme Court now held that the chancellor had

overstepped his jurisdiction by ordering an election in court. The election in court was therefore invalid and the case was remanded to the chancellor. The Supreme Court on this occasion pointed out the uselessness of the litigation, expressing the opinion that a trustee merely holding the legal title to the church property should not be confused with trustees elected or appointed to exercise active duty in controlling the affairs of the congregation, and that the litigation was entered upon because of this confusion.

When the case went back to the lower court, the chancellor again ordered a reconveyance to the bishop, but the case was again appealed.

The Supreme Court now held that the congregation either totally misapprehended the law regarding ownership of church property or that it was consciously attempting to evade the law; in either case it had no relief in equity. Regarding the office of trustee the court said:

"The office of trustee simply of legal title is not created by ecclesiastical authority, but created by the law. Such trustee can exercise no control whatever over the property held in trust. Being an officer created by law, and answerable only to the law, he can derive neither authority or power from any other source. His duties, privileges, authority and responsibility, *qua* trustee, can neither be enlarged or impaired by ecclesiastical interference, and any attempt to so interfere would be quite as illegal as though forbidden in express terms."

With the interdict still on the church, because the trustees refused to reconvey the property to the bishop, and the courts would not compel them to do so, the congregation was deprived of services in its church. Some of the recalcitrants then secured the services of a priest out of communion with the Church. Faithful members of the congregation thereupon brought action to enjoin this priest from using the church. The injunction was granted by the chancellor, but the matter was again carried to the Supreme Court.

The Supreme Court on this occasion held that the injunction was an attempt to do indirectly what could not have been done directly, and that those seeking the injunction were not entitled to equitable relief.[17] Relief should be sought by asking the ecclesiastical authorities to remove the interdict.

The bishop now revoked the interdict and reinstated the trustees. The schismatic worship was continued in the church, but the injunction against it was now upheld by the Supreme Court because the objection to the injunction had been removed.

While the holding of property by the bishop in trust for the Church is thus almost equivalent to making the bishop the mere agent of the court in the administration of the property, and while this method of tenure is apt to occasion interference on the part of the laity, it is questionable whether these two objections have very great weight. The courts in this country are generally favorable to the Church, and there is apt to be little interference on the part of the people, particularly if the prescriptions of the Code are put into effect. In places where the trust is not mentioned in the deed and where at the same time it is certain that the courts would declare a trust to exist in case the property of the church should be endangered, the decisions show that there is less possibility of the courts permitting lay interference. Interference of this kind is an exceptional thing at the present time, and perhaps the possibility of it should be risked in order to insure the protection of the courts over property in trust for religious purposes.

[17] It must be understood that this decision of the court did not give the recalcitrants a right to have schismatic service. The court merely refused to give the plaintiff any relief. It is a principle of equity that he who seeks equity must do equity; and the court in this case was of the opinion that the plaintiff was endeavoring to compel the trustees to do what the courts refused to command them to do.

CHAPTER IX.

THE BISHOP AS A CORPORATION SOLE.

"The bishop will be able to become a corporation sole before the law, to hold and administer the property of the whole diocese."[1]

"Corporations sole," says Blackstone,[2] "consist of one person only and his successors, in some particular station, who are incorporated by law, in order to give them some legal capacities and advantages, particularly that of perpetuity, which in their natural capacities they could not have had. In this sense the King is a sole corporation; so is a bishop; so are some deans and prebendaries, distinct from their several chapters; and so is every parson and vicar. And the necessity, or at least use, of this institution will be very apparent if we consider the case of the parson of a church. At the original endowment of parish churches, the freehold of the church, the church-yard, the parsonage-house, the glebe, and the titles of the parish were vested in the then parson by the bounty of the donor, as a temporal recompense to him for his spiritual care of the inhabitants, and with intent that the same emoluments should ever afterward continue as a recompense for the same care. But how was this to be effected? The freehold was vested in the parson; and if we suppose it vested in his natural capacity, on his death it might descend to his heir and would be liable to his debts and encumbrances; or, at least the heir might be compellable, at some trouble and expense, to convey those rights to the succeeding incumbent. The law, therefore, has wisely ordained that the parson *quatenus* parson, shall never die, any more than the King, by making him and his successors a corporation. By which means, all the original rights of the parsonage are preserved entire to the successor; for the present incumbent, and his prede-

[1] Concl. Plenarium Balt. III, Tit. IX, cap. ii, n. 267.
[2] o. c., I, 470.

cessor who lived seven centuries ago, are in law one and the same person, and what was given to the one was given to the other also."

This form of corporation, according to Blackstone, is a distinctly English conception of the persona moralis.[3] "Tres faciunt collegium" was the maxim of the Roman lawyers,[4] although their law permitted a corporation once established to exist as long as a single member survived;[5] in the corporation sole there is never more than one member at a time. Nor is the corporation sole to be confused with the so-called Roman institution: the latter was composed of no physical persons, but of inanimate objects; the former is composed, if the term may be used, of a single physical person. The corporation sole is therefore an anomaly.[6]

The anomaly appears to be all the more curious if we examine the tenure of property by the corporation sole. There can be no doubt that the corporation held the property in fee simple.[7] Moreover, "At the original endowment . . . the freehold of the Church . . . was vested in the then parson" but "as a temporal recompense for the spiritual care of the inhabitants with the intent that the same emoluments should ever afterward continue as a recompense for the same care."[8] The deed, by which the property was granted, conveyed a fee simple. The grantee in the deed was the then parson. Nevertheless the then parson did not possess the fee simple to the property; he had a freehold estate, but not of inheritance. The parson's tenure was therefore similar to a trust, though it was not a trust since the limitations upon it were created by law.

---

[3] o. c., I, 469.

[4] D. 50, 18, 8.

[5] D. 3, 4, 7, 2.

[6] It might be asked whether canon law has adopted the corporation sole. In canon 100, e. g., the Holy See is designated as a persona moralis. "Utrum autem sustinens denominationem personae moralis sit ipsum officium supremum regendi, ipsa sedes cui tale officium cohaeret, an persona moralis sit consideranda in serie personarum ut eadem perseverat in quolibet membro succedente, est res disputabilis" (Wernz-Vidal, o. c., Vol. II, p. 31). "Est potius res quam persona" is the opinion of Cocchi (Commentarium in Codicem Iursis Canonici, Lib. II, Pars I, Sectio I, p. 31).

[7] Blackstone, o. c., II, 108.

[8] Blackstone, I, 470.

Maitland[9] therefore asks the question: "Is a beneficed clergyman, for instance, the Rev. John Styles, a corporation sole, or is he merely the administrator or representative of a corporation sole?" "The parson," he says, "had the fee *in iure Ecclesiae* as one is seized in fee *in iure uxoris suae,* and yet, for some purposes he is only a tenant for life."

If Maitland's theory is correct, the parson was not the corporation sole but merely its administrator and a tenant for life in the property of which the corporation sole was seized. The corporation sole is then merely a collection of goods personified by the law—the foundation or institution of modern Roman jurists. "The canonist will subjectify the Church. The Church (subject) owns the Church (object). . . . What is the relation of the ecclesia particularis to the universal church? Are we to think of a persona ficta, or a patron saint, or of the bride of Christ, or of that vast corporation aggregate, the congregatio omnium fidelium, or of Christ's vicar at Rome, or of Christ's poor throughout the world; or shall we say that the walls are capable of retaining possession?" In another place he says: "As a garden belongs to a house, as a stopper belongs to a bottle, not as a house and bottle belong to a man, so the glebe belongs to the Church."[10]

If Maitland's theory were true, the corporation sole in the individual parish would be the ideal repository of the legal title to parochial property, since it would be the exact equivalent of the persona moralis that holds property under canon law. But regardless of what the theory might have been originally, the fact is that the law now follows Blackstone in considering the parson as the solitary member of the corporation sole and not merely as its administrator.

Traces of the corporation sole were to be found in early American law, both in the states having the Congregational system, and in the states where the worship of the Church of England was in vogue; but when these states ceased to have an established form of worship, the corporation sole gradually disappeared.

[9] Maitland: *The Corporation Sole;* The Law Quarterly Review, Vol. XVI, p. 335.

[10] Maitland seems to insinuate that the corporation sole was an invention of ecclesiastics to deprive the patron of the title that was originally in him.

In Congregational states, such as Maine and Massachusetts, corporations sole existed as part of the territorial parish system.[11] In these states, originally, the ecclesiastical and civil territories were identical, and officers of the township provided for the ecclesiastical, as well as the mundane needs of the people,[12] while parish affairs were transacted at political meetings of the township.[13] The minister held the parsonage and other lands granted for the use of himself or his ministry, but he held them, in the right of the town or parish, to himself and his successors. When a vacancy occurred, the town was entitled to the custody of the property and to the profits accruing from it until the vacancy was filled.[14] While the minister as corporation sole was deemed to be seized of the lands in fee simple, he was also said to have them in the right of the parish or township.[15] The town could not alienate the lands without the consent of the minister. The minister could alienate, but the alienation would be valid only as long as he should remain minister. If, however, both minister and parish, or vestry, should sell the property, the alienation would bind the successor.[16] The territorial parish gradually disappeared, and with it, the form of corporation sole which it supported.[17]

In Virginia, where the Established Church of England was adopted, the minister was also a corporation sole, governed by the common law of England so far as it was applicable to the colony.[18] In this state, since there was no dependence on the congregational system, the process of elimination was quite different from that of Maine and Massachusetts. By statute passed in 1802, it was provided that the title to lands held by Episcopal ministers, as corporations sole, should upon the death of the then present incumbents, be vested in the Overseers of the Poor. The

---

11 Zollmann, o. c., 43, 44.

12 Ibid., 39.

13 Austin v. Thomas, 14 Mass., 338.—Lincoln, o. c., 443.

14 Brunswick v. Dunning, 7 Mass., 445; Weston v. Hunt, 2 Mass., 500.—Lincoln, o. c., 438, 441.

15 Weston v. Hunt, 2 Mass., 500.

16 Weston v. Hunt, 2 Mass., 500.

17 Zollmann, *American Civil Church Law,* 39–43.

18 Tennett v. Taylor, 9 Cranch (U. S.) 43.—Lincoln, o. c., 571.

constitutionality of the statute was contested, but upheld by the lower court. The case was carried to the Supreme Court. The judges of the Supreme Court stood three to two for a reversal, but the night before the decision was to be rendered, one of the judges in the majority died and the decision of the court of original jurisdiction was consequently upheld. When, at a later period, the question again came before the Supreme Court, the judges preferred to let the former decision remain unchanged, because it had been recognized by all branches of the government, and most of the Church lands had been alienated under it. The statute did not operate to dissolve the corporation sole until the death of the then present incumbents, but those incumbents have all passed away, and in Virginia today there is no such entity as the corporation sole.[19]

Outside of the original colonies there have been a few instances where courts have decided that the position of the Catholic priest of a mission was analogous to that of a sole corporation in England,[20] thus creating quasi-corporations sole without legislative authority. The general rule, however, is that a priest or a bishop has no corporate rights, unless he obtains them from the state, by incorporating under the enabling act of the legislature. The corporation sole is, like all other corporations in America, a creature of the law.

Attempts have been made to induce the various state legislatures to pass statutes enabling bishops to become corporations sole, but the law makers seem to have objected, on the ground that this would be a form of special privilege, the Roman Catholic Church being practically the only one to profit by it. Some states, however, have passed statutes authorizing bishops of various denominations to become corporations sole by complying with certain stipulated conditions, extremely simple to execute.[21]

To give a critique of the corporation sole as it exists today would be extremely temerous. The law by which

---

[19] Zollmann, o. c., 44, 45.

[20] In Illinois, Kentucky, Texas, California, and Georgia. See 14 Corpus Juris, 71; Zollmann, o. c., 46.

[21] California, Connecticut, Kentucky, Illinois, Massachusetts, and Maryland; Zollmann, o. c., 46.

it is governed is purely statutory, and decisions interpreting these statutes are very rare.[22] How much bearing the common law would have on the interpretation of the statutes is a matter of conjecture, particularly since the episcopal corporation sole vested with the title to all parochial property is something hitherto unknown. Kent says[23] that there are few points of corporation law applicable to the corporation sole; and this fact renders the matter all the more difficult. We may, however, submit a few queries which, if they could be decided by a glance at the statutes of the individual states, would throw some light on the desirability of this method of tenure:

(1) Would it be necessary for the bishop, under this system of tenure, to make a will in favor of his successor in order to prevent the movable goods of the Church from passing to his heirs? Corporations sole could not, according to English law, take personal property in succession, and their corporate capacity in this respect was confined to real property.[24] This matter could, however, be regulated by statute.

(2) Does the corporation sole, in the particular state, hold the property to itself, or in trust for another? For corporations sole are of two kinds: the one so constituted that the parson has a corporate capacity for his own benefit; the other, so that he acts only as trustee for the benefit of others. The statute alone could not decide this question.

(3) If the corporation sole is a mere trustee, can it be forced by the *cestui qui trust* to convey its trust to another as in the Pennsylvania case reviewed in the last chapter?

(4) Presuming that the corporation sole is not a trustee, would it be able to part with the fee without the consent of the parish or the diocese?

Aside from these difficulties, the corporation sole offers a safe method of holding church property. It forever protects the Church's title by passing it from the predecessor to the successor without any formalities except proof of

[22] This is perhaps a point in favor of the corporation sole. The fact that little or no trouble has arisen under this system of tenure at least indicates that the system is workable.

[23] Kent, *Commentaries,* II, 273.

[24] Kent, *Commentaries,* II, 273.—14 Corpus Juris, 71.

the fact of succession. It also leaves the bishop free to administer the property according to the canons of the Church, since a corporation sole, like a physical person, can act officially either by itself or through an agent. The one great disadvantage that it entails is that when a bishop dies or resigns his office, the fee is in abeyance, until a successor is appointed, and no one during the interregnum is duly qualified to transact business.[25]

[25] 14 Corpus Juris, 71.

CHAPTER X.

THE CORPORATION AGGREGATE.

The modes of tenure so far discussed were, according to the mind of the Third Plenary Council of Baltimore, to apply only "in the states in which a civil incorporation of parishes or ecclesiastical bodies, such as accords with church law, does not exist."[1] Strictly speaking, such an incorporation can never exist under our laws, since the title to church property under canon law is vested in a *persona moralis non-collegialis,* and this form of moral person does not exist in the United States; but the council ostensibly had in mind a corporation which, while not identical in theory with the ecclesiastical moral person, practically functions in the manner prescribed by the sacred canons. That this is the corporation aggregate is clear from the decree of the Sacred Congregation of the Council, July 29, 1911.[2] Nevertheless, it must not be supposed that every form of corporation aggregate fulfills the required conditions.

In order to determine whether the required conditions are fulfilled in a given instance, it is necessary to know the provisions of the statute under which the corporation is formed; and since a statute cannot be so perfectly worded as to leave no doubt about its application to the multifarious problems that might arise under it, it is equally necessary to know how the courts of the particular state have interpreted the statute. To be more explicit, one would have to know definitely whether the corporate body is composed of trustees or of the collective membership of the congregation; whether the trustees are elected by the members, or appointed by ecclesiastical authority; whether the corporation is or is not limited as to the amount of the property it can hold; whether the trustees have the legal title to this property, or merely the right of administration;

---

[1] Concl. Plenarium Balt. III, Tit. IX, cap. ii, n. 267.

[2] Eccl. Rev., Nov., 1911, 591–596; Micheletti, *Ius Pianum,* 334, 335.

whether the corporation holds the property absolutely, or in trust for the Church; and, finally, whether the courts do, or do not consider the corporation as denominational in character. These are by no means the only considerations affecting the problem, but they are the most important.

In order to treat this problem in an exhaustive manner one would have to have access to the corporation statutes of the several states as well as to the reports of decisions growing out of them; and even then he would have to have the gift of prophecy if he wished to determine how future cases would be decided by the courts. Even to list the various corporations categorically is quite hazardous, since the freedom given by the states to religious corporations varies in degree, from Virginia and West Virginia, which do not permit them at all, to New York, which, according to the Sacred Congregation of the Council,[3] offers the most desirable form of them. It is useful, however, to have some sort of classification as a basis for discussion; and one can do no better than to adopt the classification of Zollmann[4] who distinguishes between corporations composed of trustees and those composed of the members of the congregation.[5] Nevertheless in adopting this classification, one must not lose sight of the fact that:

"The statutes in regard to religious corporations are quite frequently ambiguous and the judicial utterances are more or less vacillating between the two theories. The same court will be found to adopt now one theory, now another. Occasionally opinions are even found which adopt both, or which are written in such a way that it is impossible to say which theory is favored by the court."[6]

With this animadversion we may return to the classification:

---

[3] Ibid. The decree states that the preferable method of tenure is through the parish corporation conditioned and safeguarded as in the State of New York.

[4] o. c., 49 to 61.

[5] Zollmann really speaks of the trustee corporation and the aggregate corporation; but since the trustee corporation is composed of a plurality of persons it is a form of corporation aggregate, and there will be less confusion if we speak of the trustee corporation and the congregational corporation.

[6] Zollmann, o. c., 60.

I. The Trustee Corporation.—The trustee corporation is a development of what was spoken of in a former chapter as the trustee system. When territorial parishes went out of existence they were followed by voluntary religious societies that were not incorporated. When these societies began to accumulate property, the question of tenure presented a difficulty. The society having no legal personality could not hold the property in its own name. The members could hold it; but the membership was so large, and the personnel of the society so unstable, that tenancy in common was impractical. The societies therefore chose to elect a certain number of trustees to hold the property for the members.[7]

These trustees, being unincorporated, held the legal title in their individual names, and this was a source of untold trouble. When a trustee died the courts would have to determine the disposition of the property. This disposition depended on the nature of the trustee's estate, and only three situations were possible: (1) the trustee had only a life estate; (2) all the trustees held the fee as joint tenants; (3) all the trustees held the fee as tenants in common. Where the trustee had only a life estate, the fee reverted to the original owner; where the trustee was one of several joint tenants the fee passed to the surviving trustees, and, at the death of the last survivor, to his heirs; where the trustee was a tenant in common, his share in the property descended to his heirs. Thus, although the members of the congregation had their equity in the property, the legal title could, and sometimes did, get into the hands of incompetent trustees. Equity could at times have furnished a remedy, but the churches were loath to go into court on account of the bitter feelings that this might engender.[8]

In order to overcome the inconveniences caused by the instability of the trustees, the churches asked for special charters incorporating the trustees, and these special charters were, at a later period, supplanted by general incorporation statutes. Thus while the equitable title to the property still remained in the unincorporated society, the

[7] Zollmann, o. c., 49.

[8] Zollmann, o. c., 49, 50.

legal title was vested in a corporate body, instead of in the individual trustees. Though a trustee should die, the corporation continued to exist. Another trustee could be elected or appointed to fill the vacancy, and this process could go on indefinitely, so that the title was never in abeyance.[9]

In this respect, the trustee corporation is an improvement, not only on the trustee system, but on the corporation sole as well. To say, however, that this form of corporation is more desirable than the corporation sole, would be an ex parte conclusion. There are other facts that must be taken into consideration.

Says a court in Indiana:[10]

"The religious societies whose trustees are incorporated present a three-fold aspect; first, the congregation who usually meet together for the purpose of religious worship; second, the church strictly so-called, an ecclesiastical body composed of such persons entitled to church privileges; third, the legal corporate body composed of the board of trustees, each of them acting separately."

In other words, there are three distinct societies: the first is a voluntary association based upon a multilateral contract among the members of the parish, and having no rights apart from the individual rights of the members; the second is a spiritual society whose authority over its members, in religious matters, the court will recognize, although it has no personality in private law; the third is a corporation, a creature of the law, possessing personality, and acting as agent and trustee for one or both of the other societies. It is, therefore, not difficult to understand how this arrangement can give rise to many complicated problems.

In the matter of making contracts it would seem that the trustee corporation is the only body recognized by the courts. The trustees, in their corporate capacity, have full control over the civil relations of the Church. A pastor cannot legally take charge of a parish unless appointed, or approved, by them, and to them he must look for the

---

[9] Zollmann, o. c., 51.

[10] Gray v. Good, 89 N. E., 498.

payment of his salary. If he proves incompetent, it is they, and they alone, who can depose him. The trustee corporation is so clearly distinct from the church, that the trustees may be non-members and even excommunicated persons.[11]

When the congregation is the reproductive organ of the trustee corporation electing the trustees, and afterwards filling the vacancies, it goes without saying, that the Catholic Church cannot afford to adopt this system. But if the enabling act of a particular state permits the trustee corporation to be composed of the bishop, the pastor, and some other church official,[12] not in their capacity as private persons, but by virtue of their office, so that their successors in office become, ipso officio, their successors as trustees, the trustee corporation would be, in most respects, a very desirable arrangement.

Further difficulties might, however, arise from the fact of trusteeship. Since the corporation is a mere trustee, there must be a cestui qui trust, and a purpose for which the trust is created. The members of the parish would, undoubtedly, constitute the cestui qui trust, and the equitable title would vest in them. How much control they might, at times, be able to exercise over the property, would be for a court of equity to determine. Zollmann,[13] in speaking of the trustees, says that "Their title is so absolutely apart from all beneficial ownership that an act of the legislature transferring it to another body has been upheld." The purpose of the trust would present but little difficulty for the Catholic Church, since her creed is, and always will be, immutable. Still, where the courts take the view that a trustee corporation is not denominational in character, it would be a wise precaution always to have the purpose of the trust clearly expressed in the deed, so that the courts would be obliged to consider not only the corporation and the congregation, but the third element, "the church strictly so-called."

II. The Congregational Corporation.—The congregational corporation is, as the name indicates, a juristic

[11] Zollmann, o. c., 52, 53.

[12] It is submitted that the vicar general should not be included. Since the vicar general loses his office when the bishop dies, a double vacancy would exist during the interregnum.

[13] o. c., p. 54.

person composed of the members of the parish. According to Zollmann, [14] it came into being as the result of certain courts adopting a new construction of religious incorporation acts. Property held by trustee corporations was held subject to certain trusts; the beneficiaries under these trusts sometimes went into court seeking equitable relief, and where these beneficiaries belonged to a Church that was independent of any synod or central governing body, it was often difficult to determine the purpose of the trust. This purpose, as a general rule, would be dependent on the belief of the congregation at the time that the property was acquired;[15] but in a congregation where there existed no unity of belief, or where the original creed had been changed, the problem of determining what the collective faith of the members had been, at a specified period in the past, was an insurmountable obstacle for the courts. This difficulty induced the courts to scrutinize the incorporation acts for some better theory. In New York it was found that the enabling act was not closely worded, the members of the parish sometimes being referred to as corporators; the court finally took advantage of this looseness of construction and held that no trust existed, the trustees being nothing more than officers of the corporation, whose corporators were the members of the parish. This theory was also adopted by some of the other states.[16]

Where the congregational corporation exists, the distinction between the corporation and "the church so-called" is still outstanding; but instead of three-fold aspect, said to exist where the trustees are incorporated, there are now only two elements to be considered:

"An incorporated Church consists of two distinct elements, to wit: the Church proper and the incorporation, which has relation only to the temporalities of the institution."[17]

What, then, is the position of the trustees in their relation to these two elements? Do they still hold the property subject to an implied trust (though the foundation of this

[14] o. c., pp. 54 to 58.

[15] Vide supra, Chapter V.

[16] Zollmann, o. c., 57.

[17] Des Mukes v. States, 50 So. (Ala.) 195.

trust has been removed by the courts), or are they merely officers, whose position is similar to the board of directors of a commercial corporation? In case a trust exists, is it merely for the benefit of the corporation, or is it also bound up with the church proper? Again, where the legal title is in the corporation (the trustees being mere officers of that body), is the title of the corporation absolute, so that the congregation could change its form of worship, and still retain the use of the property, or is the property dedicated to the use of a particular denomination?

No attempt will be made to answer these questions. They are merely set down in order to show what a complicated entity a congregational corporation may become. Courts will vary in the theories they adopt, and consistency is not always to be expected even in a particular state. "Courts," says Zollmann,[18] quoting a Missouri case, "will adopt 'such a view of the law as will permit religious bodies to be incorporated, and yet preserve their original form of Church government, instead of revolutionizing it from a hierarchical or synodical into a congregational form.' " It is worthy of note, however, that in the same case it is asserted that:

"When a corporation is formed for religious purposes, everyone who belongs to the congregation becomes, by force of the statutes, a member of the corporation, even though a few individuals are named in the charter as trustess or directors, and that the document is issued to them. A church or congregation by incorporating is constituted a civil political institution, composed of the members of the congregation, and the sovereignty of the body, so to speak, vests in and remains with the majority, regardless of whether they adhere to the orthodox faith of the sect and continue in fellowship with its synods, presbyteries, or other governing bodies, or become heretical and recusant."[19] It is therefore submitted that where a congregation is incorporated, every deed, by which property is conveyed to the corporation, should contain an express declaration of trust; and the necessity of this will further appear from the following quotation:

[18] o. c., 59.

[19] Klix v. St. Stanislaus Church, 137 Mo. App., 347; 118 S. W., 1171.

"In Illinois the trustees of an incorporated religious society do not hold the property, in the absence of a declared or, at least, clearly implied trust, for any church in general, nor for the benefit of any particular doctrines or tenets of faith and practice in religious matters, but solely for the society or congregation whose officers they are; and they are not, in the discharge of their duties, subject to the control of an ecclesiastical judicatory. The property belongs to the society or congregation so long as the corporation exists, and when it ceases to exist *the property belongs to the donors or their heirs*—and this conclusively distinguishes this property from property held in trust for the benefit of a particular religious denomination. Where property is held in trust for the benefit of a particular religious denomination, the dissolution of the local corporation can in nowise affect the trust so long as the religious denomination has an existence, for it is to it, and not to the corporation, that the use belongs."[20]

A great deal more might be written about corporations aggregate. There are, for example, limitations in some states as to the amount of property a religious corporation may hold. But, neither the scope of this thesis, nor the time allotted for its preparation, will permit a more adequate treatment. The object of the present chapter was to show what the Third Plenary Council of Baltimore had in mind when it referred to "states in which a civil incorporation of parish or ecclesiastical bodies, such as accords with canon law, does not exist"; and it is submitted that this has been shown, however superficially. While most of the states at present permit religious corporations, these corporations are frequently subject to the control of the members of the parish, by reason of the fact that these members have the right either to elect the trustees, or to interfere with their activity, with the help of the courts of equity. It now remains to be seen how this objectionable feature is sometimes eliminated.

To speak of absolute elimination of this objectionable feature would be temerous. It may be possible to induce a state legislature to pass an act of incorporation, under

[20] Calkins v. Cheney, 92 Ill., 463.

which Catholic parishes may secure a charter which would be ideal on its face, but the interpretation of the charter would, in time of litigation, be left to the courts. The courts, however, are generally desirous of seeing the laws of the Church carried out, and there is but little to fear if the incorporation act is carefully drawn up. Hence, in practice, the corporation aggregate can, with the aid of the legislature, be converted into a very safe and desirable depository of the civil title to Catholic Church property in the United States. In order to see how this can be effected, it is but necessary to examine the incorporation act of the State of New York,[21] which, according to the Sacred Congregation of the Council,[22] should serve as a model for other states to follow:

"50. Incorporation of Roman Catholic and Greek Churches.—An unincorporated Roman Catholic Church or an unincorporated Christian Orthodox Church of the Eastern Confession, in this state may become incorporated as a church by executing, acknowledging and filing a certificate of incorporation, stating the corporate name by which such church shall be known and the county, town, city or village where its principal place of worship is, or intended to be, located.

"A certificate of an incorporated Roman Catholic Church shall be executed and acknowledged by the Roman Catholic archbishop or bishop, and the vicar general of the diocese in which its place of worship is, and by the rector of the church, and by two laymen, members of such church who shall be selected by such officials, or a majority of such officials.

"On filing such certificate such church shall be a corporation by the name stated in the certificate."

The simplicity of these formalities is apparent. The mere filing of a certificate properly executed is all that is required. It is also worthy of note that the two laymen must be members of the church and must be selected by the officials, or a majority of them; this is more in accordance with canon law than if they were elected by the

[21] Cfr. Cummings and Gilbert: *Membership and Religious Corporations of New York,* 315, . . .

[22] Eccl. Rev., Nov., 1911, 591–596; Micheletti, *Ius Pianum,* 334, 335.

people.[23] The people, however, are the corporators, and the trustees simply the governing body.[24] "The trustees do not sustain to the corporation the relation of a private trustee to a cestui qui trust. They are trustees only in a sense in which the trustees of a civil corporation are such. They are its managing agents and may act for it as fully as the directors or agents of other corporate bodies."[25]

"51. Government of Incorporated Roman Catholic and Greek Churches.—The archbishop or bishop and the vicar general of the diocese to which any incorporated Roman Catholic Church belongs, the rector of such church, and their successors in office shall, by virtue of their offices, be trustees of such church. Two laymen, members of such church, selected by such officers or by a majority of them, shall also be trustees of such incorporated church, and such officers and such laymen trustees shall together constitute the board of trustees thereof. The two laymen signing the certificate of incorporation of an unincorporated Roman Catholic Church shall be the two laymen trustees thereof during the first year of its corporate existence. The term of office of the two laymen trustees of an incorporated Roman Catholic Church shall be one year. Whenever the office of such layman trustee by expiration of the term of office or otherwise, becomes vacant, his succeosor shall be appointed from the members of the church by such officers or a majority of them. No act or proceeding of the trustees of any such incorporated church shall be valid without the sanction of the archbishop or bishop of the diocese to which such church belongs, or in case of their absence or inability to act, without the sanction of the vicar general or of the administrator of such diocese."

The provisions here laid down are highly desirable. The lay trustees must be members of the church, and their term of office is one year. The officials have the right at all times to choose the lay trustees, and it would seem from the final provision that the bishop must sanction the choice. While the actual administration of the corporation is in the hands of all the trustees, their official acts, to be valid,

23 Cfr. Canons 1520, 1521.

24 Note of Cummings and Gilbert, l. c.

25 Cummings and Gilbert, o. c., 277.

must be sanctioned by the bishop; thus, harmony with canon law is again made possible.[26] In fact, perfect harmony, humanly speaking, seems to be established by certain court decisions: "Trustees of a religious corporation must administer its property according to the discipline, rules and usages of the denomination to which the church members belong and the idea that corporations formed under the act of 1813 have no denominational character is no longer tenable, and a court of equity may be invoked to restrain a diversion or attempted diversion of the corporate property from its denominational uses, whether made by the congregation or the trustees."[27]

Another desirable feature is that when the office of bishop is vacant the administrator has the bishop's power of sanction or veto. This provision makes it possible during the interregnum for the corporation to function in the same manner that it functions during the life of the bishop.

"52. Division of Roman Catholic Parish; disposition of property.—When a Roman Catholic parish has been heretofore or shall hereinafter be duly divided by the Roman Catholic bishop having jurisdiction over such parish, and the original Roman Catholic Church corporation is given one part of the old parish, and a new or second Roman Catholic corporation is given the remaining part of the old parish, and it further appears that by reason of the said division the original Roman Catholic Church corporation holds title to real property situate within the part of the old parish that was given to the new or second Roman Catholic Church corporation, then the said Roman Catholic bishop or his successor shall have the right and power, of himself, independently of any action or consent on the part of the trustees of the original Roman Catholic Church corporation, to transfer the title of the said real property, with or without valuable consideration, to the said new or second Roman Catholic Church corporation. Said transfer shall be made by the said Roman Catholic bishop or his successor after having complied with the requirements of the code of civil procedure in the same

[26] Cfr. e. g. Canon 1519, 1530, § 1, 3°; 1532, § 2; 1521, etc.

[27] Cummings and Gilbert, o. c., 271.

manner as the trustees of any religious corporation are compelled to do before making a transfer of church property. If a valuable consideration is paid for the transfer, the same shall be received by the said Roman Catholic bishop or his successor and distributed between the said original Roman Catholic Church corporation and the new or second Roman Catholic Church corporation in such proportions as in the discretion of the said bishop, or his successor, may deem proper."

These final provisions in the New York Code render the New York arrangement still more consonant with church law. The section immediately preceding this makes it invalid for the trustees to act without the approval of the bishop, but does not seem to give the bishop the right to act independently of the trustees. In the final section, however, the bishop can do this where there is a question of the division of a parish. Canon law[28] gives the bishop the right to divide a parish against the will of its rector, and without the consent of the people, and provides that in this case the assets and liabilities of the old parish be equitably distributed between the old and the new.[29] How closely the New York Code follows these provisions is apparent to the reader.

To sum up the situation in New York. Although the civil corporation through which a parish conducts its secular affairs is different in nature from the persona moralis non-collegialis which has dominion under the law of the church, this difference is due to a difference of the laws of Church and State in their respective conception of a persona moralis. In practical functioning of the civil corporation, the laws of the church can be carried out in virtue of the excellent provisions of the New York incorporation act. These provisions are rendered still more excellent by the construction which the courts have placed upon the statute.

In conclusion, it might be asked why the example set by New York has not been followed in all the other states.[30]

---

[28] Canon 1427.
[29] Canon 1500.
[30] Similar statutes do exist in some places.—See Desmond, o. c., 73, 74.

This would be very difficult for two reasons: (1) The tendency of the law at the present time is to avoid special privilege, particularly in regard to chartering corporations. Early in the history of the country each individual corporation was created by a special act of the legislature. The even increasing demand for charters threatened to prevent the legislators from performing their other duties. Besides, there was too much room for favoritism in the matter of granting a charter to one company and denying it to their competitors. This led various states to pass constitutional amendments prohibiting the legislature from issuing special charters, but providing for general incorporation acts, under which any group of citizens could obtain a charter by complying with the required conditions. These amendments affected religious corporations as well as other forms.[31] In the state of New York special privilege is avoided by giving each sect a general incorporation act consonant with its peculiar form of government.[32] (2) While an act of the legislature takes precedence over the common law, it does not take precedence over the state constitution, and the judiciary may declare the act unconstitutional, and therefore invalid.[33] It is, therefore, uncertain whether the judiciaries of other states would uphold an act similar to that of the state of New York. Furthermore, the judiciaries would construe such an act in reference to the principles of the common law; "for it is not to be presumed that the legislature intended to make any innovation upon the common law, further than the case actually required."[34] It is possible, therefore, for an incorporation act, which may appear ideal on its face, to be rendered undesirable, from the Catholic point of view, by the application of established theories in its construction.

[31] Zollmann, o. c., 65 to 67.

[32] These various acts may be found in Cummings and Gilbert, o. c.

[33] Kent, o. c., I, 449–450.

[34] Ibid., 464.

CHAPTER XI.

CONCLUSION.

While uniformity in the method of holding church property in the various states is "a consummation devoutly to be wished," it would appear, from the foregoing study, that such uniformity would be difficult to obtain, first, because of the antipathy of American legislators towards what they deem to be special privilege, and second, because of the theories that might be read into a statute by the American courts. But, presuming that these difficulties could be overcome, what recommendation should be made as to the method of tenure to be adopted?

From the standpoint of convenience in the administration of parochial property, and of perfect accord with the theories of canon law, there can be no doubt that the ideal arrangement would be the corporation sole as it existed—according to Mr. Maitland[1]—in its early English form, not with the bishop as its sole member, but by the incorporation of each individual parochial benefice. But, since this form of corporation could hardly be revived, the next best arrangement would be the parochial incorporation as it exists in the state of New York.

From the standpoint of future safety to the property of the Church, it is obvious that no recommendation can be made. Still, if a time should ever come, which God forbid, when a particular state should attempt to confiscate the property of the Church, it might be more difficult, owing to the genius of English and American law, to take away property held in the name of the bishop as an American citizen, and without any trust attached, than to confiscate trust property or property held by a corporation. It is a matter of history that the legalized robbing of the Church in England was made possible by the statutes of mortmain aimed against corporations[2] and the doctrine of

[1] Maitland, *The Corporation Sole,* Law Quarterly Review, XVI, 335.

[2] Desmond, o. c., 36.

superstitious uses, aimed against trusts;[3] and while the doctrine of superstitious uses is not recognized in the United States,[4] something of the old mortmain policy of the English law appears in the statutes of nearly half the states.[5] It is not difficult to see that, owing to the relation between English and American law it would not be utterly impossible to revive old English statutes or theories. On the other hand, to legalize the confiscation of property held by an individual citizen, without due process of law, would require a change in the Federal Constitution.[6]

So much with regard to the ideal arrangement, under ideal conditions. Regarding the ideal arrangement under conditions as they actually exist, any recommendation that one might make would be based, necessarily, on ex parte conclusions. Each diocese can best solve the problem for itself, and, undoubtedly has, in the past, on the advice of the best legal talent. Whether a change is desirable in a given diocese, owing to the development of the civil law since the time when the existing method of tenure was adopted, is again a local question.

In an attempt to obtain expert opinion on the tenure of parochial property in this country, a questionnaire was sent to each of twenty members of the legal profession, the learned counsels of bishops in various parts of the United States. The East, the West, the South, and the Central States were represented in the answers received, which numbered twelve, or sixty per cent of the total number of replies possible.

(1) The first question was, whether parochial property in the particular diocese was conveyed to the bishop in fee simple, to the bishop in trust, to the bishop as a corporation sole, or to some form of aggregate corporation.

It was found that in none of the twelve dioceses was the property conveyed to the bishop with a trust expressed in the deed. In six of these dioceses all the property was conveyed to the bishop in fee simple. In two others the the bishop had the fee to some of the property, while some

[3] Ibid., 1-39.

[4] Ibid.

[5] Ibid., 44.

[6] Fourteenth Amendment.

was held by parish corporations. Two dioceses used the corporation sole method exclusively, and the last two, the parochial corporation exclusively for parochial property.

In four of the eight dioceses where all or some of the property was held by the bishop in fee simple, it was certain that the courts considered the bishop a trustee. In the fifth it was certain from a recent decision that the courts considered the bishop as the absolute owner, although formerly it had been believed that, when called upon to decide the question, they would consider him a trustee. In the sixth and the seventh the opinion of counsel was that the courts would declare a trust if called upon to decide the question and in the eighth that they would not.

(2) The second question had reference to taxation. It was asked whether parochial property was taxable and whether such taxation could be avoided.

In two of the responses an unqualified negative answer was given to the first part of the question. The other ten responses, which differed but little in substance, made it clear that property used exclusively for religious, educational or charitable purposes, was exempt from general taxation, either by constitutional or statutory provisions. In most cases, however, it was mentioned, that the religious or educational use had to be direct, immediate, and exclusive, and that otherwise return would have to be made. Assessments for local improvements were not considered taxes within the meaning of the provisions for exemption. The terms religious and educational purposes did not apply to parochial residences, nor to residences of teaching sisters, nor, in one diocese, to a convent of Poor Clares.

It was the consensus of opinion that the taxation of non-exempt church property could be avoided only by constitutional or statutory amendments and, consequently, that the method of tenure did not affect the amount of taxes to be paid. In one case it was given as an opinion, that with the numerous laws now in force with reference to inheritance tax, or Federal estate tax, and inheritance tax in many states, it would not be advisable to have property standing in the name of the bishop personally, because passing to his successor under a will, it would be subject to the above taxes. It was not stated whether the various forms of corporation taxes would apply to churches if they became incorporated.

(3) The third question was whether the present method of tenure caused inconvenience to the Church or jeopardized her property.

In one case, where the property was held by parish corporations, no answer was given to the question. An unqualified negative answer was given in five instances; in one of these instances, the property was held by parish corporations exclusively; in two others, by the bishop exclusively, but with the certainty that the courts considered him a trustee; in a fourth, the conditions were the same as the two last mentioned cases, with the additional fact that some property was held by corporations; in the fifth case the bishop had the fee to all church property, with the probability that the courts would not consider him a trustee.

In two instances the answer was that there was no danger, but some inconvenience. In both these instances, property was held by the bishop as a corporation sole.

In one instance, where the bishop held the fee but would probably be considered a trustee, the answer was that there had been no danger or inconvenience up to date, but that this did not rule out the possibility of future complications. In another instance, where the bishop had the fee, but was considered by the courts as a trustee, it was stated that no danger or inconvenience had existed so far, but that a dishonest, or incompetent bishop might cause untold harm.

In an instance where, in addition to property held by parish corporations, there was other property held in fee by the bishop, who was a trustee in the eyes of the court, it was stated that there was possibility of legal entanglements arising and that it would be much better all around if the laws of the particular state permitted the corporation sole.

Only one unqualified positive answer was given regarding the existence of danger. This was in an instance where the property was held by the bishop in fee simple, and where the courts had ruled that no trust was attached to the property. In this instance, however, it was stated that, to the knowledge of counsel, the existing method of tenure was the only one available.

(4) The fourth question asked whether religious corporations existed in the particular state, and whether the Catholic Church if not already incorporated would profit by such incorporation.

It was found that in only one instance was it impossible to have religious corporations. This leaves but five cases to be reported, since, as has been seen, corporations either aggregate or sole, already exist in six of the twelve states that are being considered.

In one of the remaining five instances no answer was given to the question whether the Church would profit by incorporating. In another instance it was said that any answer to this question would be only a guess. In a third instance the attorney said that, in his judgment, no advantage would accrue to the Church by incorporation. In another case an article was quoted from the state constitution providing that the title to all property of religious corporations should vest in trustees, whose election should be by members of such corporation; it was pointed out that, in this case, the bishop would be without any authority over the property. In the fifth and last instance, incorporation was not to be advised because it might result in lay interference with the management and control of church property.

(5) The fifth and last question was based on a supposition. In the event that the Church should be free to hold property under any method mentioned in the first question, it was asked what method would be preferable.

In four instances, no preference was expressed. Only two attorneys preferred the corporation aggregate, and one of these added the valuable suggestion that where the state law did not permit a desirable form of corporation, it would be advisable to have a common law trust or, as some term it, the Massachusetts trust, with the property standing in the name of, say, the bishop, the vicar general, and the chancellor. Two preferred that the bishop should hold the property in fee simple, but did not state whether they had an implied trust in mind. Four attorneys preferred the corporation sole.

In answers from dioceses where all property is held in the name of the bishop, two attorneys expressed no preference, two preferred the present system, and two the corporation sole.

Where property was held in part by the bishop and in part by corporations aggregate, one attorney preferred the corporation aggregate and another the corporation sole.

Where property was held exclusively by corporations aggregate, no preference was expressed.

Where property was held exclusively by corporations sole, one attorney preferred the existing method, while another preferred the corporation aggregate.

In conclusion, it is submitted that the above survey proves the writer's contention that no general recommendation can be made regarding tenure of church property in the United States. The attorneys consulted were among the most learned members of the profession in their respective states, and the fact that they were not in agreement with regard to the ideal method of tenure seems to indicate the presence, in their respective states, of legal theories which would render one or the other form of tenure undesirable, even if permissible under a newly enacted statute. Just as garments worn by a tourist at a resort in Florida would be ill suited for a trip into the Minnesota woods, even though the law should leave him free in the choice of dress, so the civil personality through which the Church can best function in one state is not necessarily the ideal one for every other state. It is questionable, for example, whether the act for the incorporation of Catholic parishes in the state of New York, if copied verbatim into the statute books of another state, would give the Church the same advantages in the other state that she possesses in the state of New York.

Another conclusion, drawn from the entire dissertation, is that no state, no matter how fair it may be in its dealings with the Church, is able, consistently, to allow the Spouse of Christ full freedom in the use of her God-given dowry, unless it first acknowledges the principles laid down in Catholic theology for the proper relations between the spiritual and the temporal sovereign powers. The first law of activity is that a body once set in motion will move forever in a straight line unless acted upon by some external force; and this law, we believe, is applicable to the realm of jurisprudence. The American courts originally gave impetus to the theory that the Church is a voluntary association based on contract; and this theory, if not impeded by other considerations, would have totally subjected the Church to the temporal power. But an external obstacle was found in the unwillingness of the courts to interfere in strictly ecclesiastical affairs; so the courts qualified their original assertion and said that Church relationship, in matters not involving property, is not based on contract but on a higher plane.

A final conclusion is, that, if due care is taken, Catholics need not be alarmed about the security of church property. While the courts have had many opportunities to disseize the Church, they have consistently endeavored to favor her, sometimes at the expense of laying themselves open to the charge of partiality from the standpoint of iron-clad law. American Catholics have every reason to thank God for a government such as theirs, which though inaccurate in its expression of the letter of the divine law, is so equitable and unflinching in the application of its spirit. As Archbishop Ireland said on one occasion:[7]

"Of inestimable value to us is the liberty the Church enjoys under the constitution of the republic. No tyrant here casts chains around her. No concordat limits her action or cramps her energies. She is as free as the eagle upon Alpine hills—free to spread out in unrestricted flight her pinions, to soar to vast altitudes, to put into action all her native energies. The law of the land protects her in her rights, and asks in return no sacrifices for those rights; for her rights are those of American citizenship."

---

[7] Quoted from Allen Sinclair Will, *Life of Cardinal Gibbons, Archbishop of Baltimore,* I, 438.

BIBLIOGRAPHY.

Aichner, Dr. Simon. *Compendium Juris Ecclesiastici.* Brixiae, 1887.

Augustine, Charles, O.S.B., D.D. *A Commentary on the New Code of Canon Law,* 4th ed., 8 vols. St. Louis, 1921.

Baart, P. A., S.T.L., LL.D. *The Tenure of Catholic Church Property in The United States of America* (Authorized Copy). Marshall, Mich., 1900.

Bargilliat, M. *Praelectiones Juris Canonici,* 37th ed., 2 vols. Paris, 1923, 1924.

Benson, Robert Hugh. *Christ in The Church.* St. Louis, 1911.

Blackstone, Sir William, Knt. *Commentaries on The Laws of England* (Notes by John L. Wendell), 4 vols. New York, 1852.

Blat, Fr. Albertus, O.P. *Commentarium Textus Codicis Iuris Canonici,* 4 vols. Rome, 1923.

Carriere, Joseph. *De Justitia et Jure.* Paris, 1839.

Catholic Encyclopedia, 16 vols. New York, 1907–1912.

Cathrein, Victor, S.J. *Philosophia Moralis.* Friburgi, Brisgoviae, 1911.

Cavagnis, Felix S., R.E. Card. *Institutiones Iuris Publici Ecclesiastici.* Rome, 1906.

Chelodi, Ioannis. *Ius De Personis.* Trent, 1922.

Clark, William Lawrence, LL.B. *Outlines for Review of the Fundamental Principles of the Law.* New York, 1923.

Cocchi, Guidus, C.M. *Commentarium in Codicem Iuris Canonici,* 6 vols. Turin, Rome, 1924, 1925.

Cochran, Wm. C. *The Students' Law Lexicon.* Cincinnati, 1909.

Codex Iuris Canonici. Rome, 1923.

Codicis Iuris Canonici Fontes, Cura Enis Petri Card. Gasparri Editi Romae, 3 vols., 1923, 1924, 1925.

Collectanea S. Congregationis De Propoganda Fide, 2nd ed., 2 vols. Rome, 1907.

Concilii Tridentini Canones et Decreta. Taurini, 1913.

Corpus Iuris Canonici, Richter-Friedburg. Leipsic, 2 vols., 1879, 1881.

Corpus Iuris Civilis, Coloniae Munatianiae. 1781.

Cummings, R. C., and Gilbert, F. B. *Membership and Religious Corporations of New York.* Albany, 1907.

Denzinger, H. *Enchiridion Symbolorum,* Editio Decima Tertia quam paravit Clemens Bannwart, S.J. Friburg, 1921.

Desmond, Humphrey J. *The Church and The Law.* Chicago, 1898.

Fagnanus, P. *Commentaria in Libros Decretalium,* Venitiis apud Paulum Balleonium. 1697.

Fanfani, P. Ludovicus, O.P. *De Iure Parochorum.* Rome, 1924.

Ferrari, J. C. *Summa Institutionum Canonicarum.* Genoa, 1908.

Ferraris, F. Lucius. *Prompta Bibliotheca.* Paris, 1865.

Ferreres, P. Ioannis B., S.J. *Institutiones Canonicae,* 2nd ed., 2 vols. Barcinone, 1920.

Ferrini, C. *Pandette.* Milano, 1917.

Gierke, Dr. Otto. *Political Theories of The Middle Ages.* Translated with an Introduction by Frederick William Maitland. Cambridge, 1900.

Kent, James. *Commentaries on American Law,* 12th ed., 4 vols. Boston, 1884.

Lincoln, Charles Z. *The Civil Law and The Church.* New York, 1916.

Lingard, John. *The Antiquities of The Anglo-Saxon Church.* London, 1810.

———. *A History of England,* 7th ed., vol. VI. London, 1883.

MacCaffrey, James. *History of The Catholic Church in The Nineteenth Century,* 2 vols. Dublin, 1910.

Maitland, F. W. *The Corporation Sole.* Law Quarterly Review, XVI, 535, . . .

Maroto. F. *Institutiones Iuris Canonici ad Normam Novi Codicis.* Rome. 1921.

Marruchi. O. *Elements D'Archologie Chretienne.* Paris, 1899.

Moulart, Ferdinand J. *L'Eglise et L'Etat.* Louvain, 1895.

Micheletti, A. M. *Ius Pianum.* Rome, 1918.

MPG—Migne. *Patrologiae Graecae Cursus Completus.* Paris, 1857.

Navarrus. *Opera Omnia,* 6 vols. Venice, 1618.

Pollack and Maitland. *History of English Law,* 2 vols. Cambridge, 1895.

Prummer, Dominicus, O.P. *Manuale Iuris Ecclesiastici,* 2nd ed. Friburg, 1920.

Sherman, Charles Phineas. *Roman Law in the Modern World,* 3 vols. New Haven, 1922.

Smith, William. *Dictionary of Greek and Roman Antiquities.* Boston, 1854.

Sohm, Rudolph. *The Institutes of Roman Law.* Translated by James Crawford Ledlie. Oxford, 1892.

Solieri, Francesco. *Institutiones Iuris Ecclesiastici.* Rome, 1921.

Strong, Hon. William. *Relations of Civil Law to Church Polity.* New York, 1885.

Suarez, R. P. Francisci, S.J. *Opera Omnia,* Tom. 24. Paris, 1854.

Tanquerey, Ad. *Synopsis Theologiae Dogmaticae.* New York, 1914.

———. *Synopsis Theologiae Moralis et Pastoralis.* New York, 1907.

Taunton, Ethelred. *The Law of The Church.* London, 1906.

Thomae Aquinatis. *Summa Theologica,* 6 vols. Rome, 1894.

Vidal, P. P. Petri, S.J. *Ius Canonicum Auctore P. Francisco Xav. Wernz, S.J., ad Codicis Normam Exactum,* Vol. II. Rome, 1923.

Vering. F. H. *Droit Canon,* Traduction de L'Abbe P. Belet, in *Bibliotheque Theologique du XIX Siecle.* Paris, 1881.

Vermeersch, A., S.J., and Creusen, J., S.J. *Epitome Iuris Canonici,* 2nd ed., 3 vols. Mechlin-Rome, 1926.

Wernz, F. X., S.J. *Ius Decretalium,* 2nd ed., Vol. III. Rome, 1901.

Will, Allen Sinclair. *Life of Cardinal Gibbons, Archbishop of Baltimore.* New York, 1922.

Woywod, Stanislaus, O.F.M. *The New Canon Law.* New York, 1918.

———. *A Practical Commentary on The Code of Canon Law.* New York. 1925.

Zollmann, Carl, LL.B. *American Civil Church Law.* New York, 1917.

UNIVERSITAS CATHOLICA AMERICAE

WASHINGTON, D. C.

FACULTAS JURIS CANONICI

1925-1926

No. 31

DEUS LUX MEA

THESES

QUAS

AD DOCTORATUS GRADUM

IN

JURE CANONICO

APUD UNIVERSITATEM CATHOLICAM AMERICAE

CONSEQUENDUM
PUBLICE PROPUGNABIT

CASTRENSIS JOSEPHUS BARTLETT, A. M., LL. B., J. C. L.

SACERDOS DIOECESIS CLEVELANDENSIS
HORA IX-XI A. M. DIE XXVII MAII A. D. MCMXXVI

ROMAN LAW.

I. The Three Chief Periods in the Development of Roman Law.
II. The Books of the Corpus Iuris Civilis considered as to Source and Content.
III. The Family, the Unit of Roman Society.
IV. Slavery in the Classical Period.
V. Manumission from Slavery.
VI. Legal Personality in Roman Law.
VII. Loss of Status (Capitis Diminutio) and Its Effects.
VIII. Personality of Corporations and Institutions.
IX. Titles to Property under the Ius Gentium.
X. Mancipatio and the Nature of Res Mancipi.

INTERNATIONAL LAW.

XI. Nature, Division and Scope of International Law.
XII. Sources of International Law.
XIII. Recognition of New States.
XIV. Acquisition of Territorial Jurisdiction.
XV. Jurisdiction over Vessels.
XVI. Piracy and International Law.
XVII. The Monroe Doctrine.
XVIII. The Drago Doctrine.
XIX. Consuls.
XX. Concordats.

ECCLESIASTICAL LAW.

XXI. De Iure in Genere, eiusque Divisione.
XXII. De Forma Regiminis Ecclesiae.
XXIII. De Societate Civili relate ad Ecclesiam.
XXIV. De Iuribus Ecclesiae quoad Bona Temporalia.

XXV.	Canones 8-11	De Promulgatione Legis Canonicae.
XXVI.	Canones 12-14	De Legis Canonicae Subiecto.
XXVII.	Canones 15-16	De Legibus Irritantibus et Inhabilitantibus.
XXVIII.	Canones 17-20	De Legis Canonicae Interpretatione.
XXIX.	Canones 87-89	De Hominis Personalitate in Ecclesia.
XXX.	Canones 99-102	De Persona Morali in Ecclesia.
XXXI.	Canones 329-331	De Episcoporum Nominatione.
XXXII.	Canones 332-334	De Episcoporum Provisione Canonica.
XXXIII.	Canones 335-337	De Potestate Episcoporum Residentialium.
XXXIV.	Canon 338	De Episcoporum Obligatione Residentiae.
XXXV.	Canones 343-346	De Obligatione Visitandi Dioecesim.
XXXVI.	Canones 506-507	De Electione Superioris.
XXXVII.	Canones 519-523	De Speciali Religiosae Confessario.
XXXVIII.	Canones 531-537	De Bonis Temporalibus Religiosorum.
XXXIX.	Canones 539-541	De Postulatu.
XL.	Canones 547-551	De Dote Monialium.
XLI.	Canones 727-730	De Simonia.
XLII.	Canones 745-754	De Subiecto Baptismi.
XLIII.	Canones 814-819	De Missae Ritibus et Ceremoniis.

XLIV.	Canones 820-823	De Tempore et Loco Missae Celebrandae.
XLV.	Canon 840	De Iure Celebrantis ad Integrum Stipendium.
XLVI.	Canones 845-851	De Ministro Sacrae Communionis.
XLVII.	Canones 893-900	De Reservatione Peccatorum.
XLVIII.	Canones 1250-1254	De Abstinentia et Ieiunio.
IL.	Canones 1553-1554	De Iudicii Ecclesiastici Natura et Obiecto.
L.	Canones 1556-1558	De Incompetentia Absoluta.
LI.	Canones 1706-1710	De Libello Litis Introductorio.
LII.	Canones 1747-1749	De Probationibus in Genere.
LIII.	Canones 1792-1805	De Testimonio Peritorum.
LIV.	Canon 1990	De Modo Speciali Declarandae Nullitatis.
LV.	Canones 2195-2198	De Natura Delicti.
LVI.	Canones 2212-2213	De Conatu Delicti.
LVII.	Canones 2215-2217	De Poenarum Notione et Speciebus.
LVIII.	Canones 2236-2240	De Poenarum Remissione.
LIX.	Canones 2241-2242	De Notione Censurae.
LX.	Canones 2255-2256	De Censu 'is in Specei.

Vidit Faxcultas Iuris Canonici:

PHILIPPUS BERNARDINI, S.T.D., J.U.D., Decanus.
LUDOVICUS H. MOTRY, S.T.D., J.C.D., a Secretis.
VALENTINUS T. SCHAAF, O.F.M., J.C.D.
FRANCISCUS LARDONE, S.T.D., J.U.D.
MANUEL DE OLIVIERA LIMA, L.L.D.

Vidit Facultas Iuris Canonici:

THOMAS J. SHAHAN, S.T.D.

BIOGRAPHICAL NOTE.

Chester Joseph Barlett, born at Cleveland, Ohio, on March 17, 1891, was graduated successively from Holy Name Parochial School, St. Ignatius High School and St. Ignatius College, now known as John Carroll University, Cleveland, Ohio, receiving the degree of Bachelor of Arts in June, 1912. In September, 1912, he began the study of law at Cleveland Law School of Baldwin-Wallace University, Berea, Ohio. Two years later, he received the degree of Master of Arts from St. Ignatius College, the subject of his dissertation being "Municipal Corporations for Profit." The following year he received the degree of Bachelor of Laws from Baldwin-Wallace University, and, upon passing the state bar examination, was admitted to practice in the state of Ohio, in July, 1915.

In September, 1915, he entered St. Bernard's Seminary, Rochester, New York, and was transferred the following year to St. Mary's Seminary at Cleveland, where he completed his studies in the sacred sciences, and was ordained to the priesthood by the Right Reverend John P. Farrelly, Bishop of Cleveland, on May 29, 1919.

He spent the next three years as a curate at St. Ignatius Church, Cleveland, Ohio, and the two following years as a curate at the Church of Our Lady of Mount Carmel, Warren, Ohio.

In October, 1924, he entered the School of Canon Law in the Catholic University of America, qualified for the Baccalaureate in Canon Law and attended the lectures of Doctors Filippo Bernardini, Valentine Theodore Schaaf, and Hubert Louis Motry on Canon Law, of Doctor Francesco Lardone on Roman Law, and of Doctor Manoel de Oliviera Lima on International Law. In June, 1925, he received the degree of Licentiate in Canon Law, the subject of his dissertation being "Fundamental Considerations Affecting the Tenure of Church Property in the United States of America." In order to qualify for the Doctorate in Canon Law, he wrote the present thesis.

www.ingramcontent.com/pod-product-compliance
Lightning Source LLC
LaVergne TN
LVHW050200080826
844660LV00012B/324

* 9 7 8 0 8 1 3 2 2 2 2 1 9 *